HAUNTED
DERRY

Madeline McCully

The
History
Press
Ireland

To my husband Thomas
for his love, support and encouragement
and the endless cups of tea.

First published 2015

The History Press Ireland
50 City Quay
Dublin 2
Ireland
www.thehistorypress.ie

© Madeline McCully, 2015

The right of Madeline McCully to be identified as the Author
of this work has been asserted in accordance with the
Copyright, Designs and Patents Act 1988.

British Library Cataloguing in Publication Data.
A catalogue record for this book is available from the British Library.

ISBN 978 1 84588 868 8

Typesetting and origination by The History Press

CONTENTS

FOREWORD

As a contributor to this book, with a recent tale of my own to tell, I am glad to provide this preface to Madeline McCully's excellent *Haunted Derry*.

Reading through these accounts of supernatural sightings, I'm struck by the way the past still eerily echoes in our present. Madeline has done a lot of digging into background detail and the supporting chapter and verse she includes here vividly enliven the stories she recounts in the book. Not only do we learn about the hauntings themselves, but Madeline is often in a position to tell us who these beings are, as they appear, with their old-fashioned clothes, in suddenly icy rooms. And she explains the where and the when, and often the who, so well. It puts the reader in a position to ask the question that intrigues me the most: why? That is a question about which we can only speculate. Why do these ghostly figures, encountered on wobbly stairs or woodland paths, have to linger on, reminding us, or even re-enacting incidents, of times long gone?

I hadn't realised, until I read these spectral stories, how many old gentry houses there are still in the city and its environs. In some cases they have been turned into schools or hotels, and their original owners are probably mystified, or even angered, by what's going on in these buildings now. No wonder they still make the occasional physical appearance to put manners on us. Perhaps there is a sense of ghostly satisfaction in all this. They enjoy seeing the effect they still have on us, witnessing our astonishment or terror. Or maybe they can't bear to leave us, here in the most beautiful city in Ireland, with its wide walls perched on the central hill and the great river below.

And how the history of this place echoes through these pages! This place of strife and struggle, sieges and slaughter! The old soldiers and the seafarers, the servants and the masters live in this book as truly as they seem to live among us still. And as someone who has his own tale to tell in this volume, I can testify to the truth of that statement.

Eamon Friel
BBC Radio presenter, singer and songwriter.
Derry, 2015

ACKNOWLEDGEMENTS

I have so many people to thank that I apologise in advance if I leave out anyone.

I would like to thank Doreen McBride for pointing me in the direction of writing this book and Beth Amphlett and Ronan Colgan for their belief that it could actually be done in the time available.

Thanks to Jim McCallion of the North-West Regional College for his endless patience and knowledge in preparing the photographs and to all of those who supplied photographs and research items: the McDonald/Bigger Collection, National Trust, Springhill House, Limavady Council Development Initiative, Colin Knox of Prehen House and all the other contributors.

I would particularly like to thank Maura Craig, Linda Ming and Jane Nicholson of the Central Library for their encouragement and support all the way through. The Shantallow Library staff in Derry were ever happy to help; my gratitude also goes to Ken McCormack for his words of wisdom and to the Derry Playhouse Writers, my nurture group, for believing in me.

Thanks to Derry City Council and their staff at the Tower Museum for their courtesy and interest.

I wish also to thank the Arts Council, NI, for the many ways in which they helped me fund my 'gathering of stories' over the years.

Many of those who contributed stories wished to remain anonymous and I respect that, therefore I will thank all of you for taking the time to tell me your tales and allowing me to use them. I hope that I have done them justice.

I must mention three wonderful people: Bertie Bryce, one of the truly amazing storytellers of Ireland, Sheila Quigley, founder of the Derry Yarnspinners and Pat Mulkeen, a storyteller, writer and dramatist. They greatly influenced me and gave me a love of storytelling. All unfortunately have passed on but they are not forgotten.

INTRODUCTION

UNTIL I was 12 we did not have a television in our house so it was inevitable that there would be many tales told, especially at night when the fire glowed on our childish faces and we begged for a story. At home my siblings and I heard no frightening ones but, when the darker nights came in and Halloween was just around the corner, I listened avidly to the ghost stories that other children told. We sat on a wall at the top of our street within sight of home and frightened ourselves as the stories became wilder and scarier. If there was a breeze at all, the sighs and groans of trees across the road added to the eerie atmosphere.

We lived in a small cul-de-sac of fourteen houses and our house was at the bottom, in the corner. I remember that, when I was about 8 years old, I was terrified by the story of 'the wee white woman' who came to haunt our street. According to John, one the young boys, the ghost entered through our back garden and lingered behind the hedge, waiting for us to appear. I was too afraid to go home and, much to the amusement of the boys, sat down on the pavement at the top of the street and cried.

I must have sounded like the banshee because a neighbour, Mrs Carlin, came out and scolded the boys before taking me by the hand and walking me back to my house. When she handed me over to my mother she whispered something and before I went to bed I was given a nice warm cup of Ovaltine and a ginger nut biscuit. My mother tucked me in, told me that my guardian angel would protect me and left the light on. Since then I have heard many tales about the wee white woman and to this day I can still taste the Ovaltine and ginger nuts.

My great-aunt lived in a little cottage in the country without electricity and running water. When it got too dark to see she lit the Tilley lamp in the kitchen, but going to bed at night when we stayed with her we had a candle on a saucer. The gloom outside of the candle's glow could be frightening and the corner where the coats hung could have housed ghosts waiting to come out when we lay down. It didn't help that neighbours often came around and inevitably ghost stories mingled with the gossip. Even though we weren't supposed to listen, the allure of being frightened overcame our reluctance and I remember pulling the blankets over my head and fervently saying my prayers.

I have always had a fascination with ghost stories. There is something about being pushed outside the realm of reality to a different space and feeling the scary tingle on the back of my neck that I just cannot resist. But when people ask me, 'Do you believe in ghosts?' I have to say that I don't disbelieve. I have never seen one but I have had, on occasion, a feeling of dejà vu and at times one of something or someone being nearby. I have had premonitions once or twice, but the first thing that most of us do is to try to explain things away logically or convince ourselves that it was simply imagination. I don't think we can always do that, so, for now, the 15 per cent of me that needs proof is quite content not to have it thrust upon myself.

What I can say, without any doubt whatsoever, is that those who shared their experiences with me were utterly convinced and convincing when they told me about them. Many of these people are in professions that require sifting through facts to get to the truth. It was listening to their stories and similar ones that I have come from total disbelief to the stage at which I find myself now.

In 2001 I embarked on a one-year multimedia course in the Nerve Centre in Derry. The students were invited to compete for a Commedia Award with the Millennium Commission. Together with two of my colleagues, Christiane Kuhn-McGuffin and Raymond Brady, I decided to build a website aptly named www.derryghosts.com. I gathered the stories and took the photographs and my two friends expertly did all the technical stuff. I spoke to many, many people who shared their experiences, glad that someone would listen and that they would be published. Our website won an award and thanks to Christiane and Raymond it is still online.

When I was asked what I was writing and answered 'ghost stories', the person asking usually answered with another question: 'Have you written about …?' I've always listened and there are many notes in my filing cabinet with stories that could not be included in this volume. I thank all of those who gave them to me; someday, some way, the stories will be retold. After all, I am a storyteller.

1

THE BIG HOUSES

STATELY mansions stand derelict all over Ireland. Ghostly histories are embedded in their very walls and ruins. Their isolation allows these stories to be passed down from generation to generation, and though we cringe and feel afraid we acknowledge that they are part of our heritage.

Even those that still stand have a fascination for us, and if there is not a story we are not averse to weaving one.

The Ghost of Balliniska House

Balliniska House on the Northland Road was the childhood home of James (not his real name), a man from a well-known and respected family in the city. The house (*Baile an Uisce* – townland of the water) was named after the area, which was known to have many springs (names describing the area are common in Celtic countries such as Ireland, Scotland and Wales). Balliniska was a lovely looking house, with bay windows at each side of the front door, and the event that James describes took place in his bedroom on the top-left room of the second floor.

The house was in a secluded location, sheltered by trees with a driveway curving from the Northland Road to swing along the side of the house to the front. Unfortunately, like many lovely houses, it was demolished and the plot was developed as part of a Science Park. Technology firms now occupy the newly built industrial estate. Consequently its history is lost to this generation, except perhaps in stories told by the people who once resided there.

The following story about the ghost that haunted his house is in James's own words:

We were getting one of the bedrooms upstairs redecorated and when the old wallpaper was stripped off we discovered that there were several magnificent portraits painted on the wall beneath. Our neighbour, who knew the history of the area well, said that Percy French painted them on one of his sojourns in Derry. The house used to be owned by a Judge Osborne and Percy French was a frequent visitor. He stayed in the front bedroom where he painted these pictures. The judge declared that the song 'The Mountains of Mourne' was composed in that particular bedroom as Percy looked out on Scalp Mountain and not, as is commonly believed, while looking at the Mountains of Mourne at all. The room faced north-eastwards, down towards the Buncrana Road, so he would have had a very clear view of the Donegal Hills, which fact gives the statement credence.

I would have been about 13 years of age and I slept in the room where Percy French did these paintings. I remember lying in bed early one summer's morning at about half-past five and it was quite bright. I wasn't waking out of a dream; I was wide awake and when I turned, there at the side of the bed looking straight at me was a figure. I remember it as if it was yesterday. He was very tall, with a long face and a beard. I looked down and when I did, I was shocked to see that below the knees there was nothing. I could see the carpet clearly where there should have been legs and feet. I looked again thinking that I was imagining things but there was still nothing. I screamed and cried and a maid came running in. She took me out of the bedroom, still shivering with fright and I stayed downstairs until my parents came down. I tried to tell them what had happened, but although my mother and father said nothing about the incident I never slept in that bedroom again. As far as I was aware at that time, that was the only incident and I was the only one in the family that saw this ghost.

But then, much later, when my own boys were teenagers, they would have gone to stay in that house with my father. He allocated them a different room so they would not have slept in that bedroom. During the night

Balliniska House, where Percy French once stayed in the top front bedroom, known to be haunted by the eerie figure of a man.

they were both wakened from their sleep. Both quite clearly heard footsteps coming up the stairs, but when my older boy opened the door and looked out no one was there. These boys were teenagers who would not have been easily scared but after this happened on other occasions they absolutely refused to stay in Balliniska House again. It was something that the family did not discuss. It was just accepted that things happened and life goes on.

Other pieces of information were said in passing at the time but we put no importance on them. For instance, apparently after the death of Mary Anne Knox [see p.26], the coach in which she had met her death was housed for a time in one of the barns within the land of Balliniska at the request of the Corporation. Perhaps the appearance of the ghost had something to do with that. We'll never know.

When the house was sold to a builder and developer, that was the end of that, or so we thought. I remember the next incident; although it didn't happen to me personally, it confirmed everything that I had known and experienced.

I was out hunting and shooting with a friend who had introduced the developer to me, when his phone rang. It was the new owner and he said, 'You are never going to believe this, but I was in the house today checking around and I saw a ghost.' Now this man was a purchaser, a total outsider and complete stranger who had just gone in to look the house over. It was in the day time and he was adamant that it was no trick of his imagination.

'A tall man was on the landing. I can't say that he was standing because he seemed to float because there was nothing below the knees.'

A long time later our family brought it out into the open and discussed it and my sister, who also had her own terrifying story to tell, decided to ask my father's secretary if he had ever mentioned anything about seeing ghosts. Mrs B did not reply.

We believe that he had told her but he and my mother had never, ever said anything to us. Perhaps they didn't want to frighten us so in many ways we just accepted things.

It was our home.

Strange Happenings at Balliniska House

Grace had lived most of her life in Balliniska House. She came in 1943 and left there in 2006 but in all that period there were only two instances where she was aware of some supernatural presences. The first was in 2000.

The house was very big and had a huge landing area. Grace went up the stairs one night; the light was on and the landing was all lit up. The little cat, generally a placid, timid little thing, was standing on the landing and its fur was straight out like that of a porcupine. Grace had never seen the like of it before in her life.

'Now, it is said that animals can be very sensitive to spirits and it convinced me that there must be something there. This little cat stood absolutely motionless, as if it was paralysed with fright.' Grace felt something or someone move swiftly by her and the air felt so icy cold that she began to tremble involuntarily. The cat stared at her with wide, unblinking eyes and Grace believed that they must be in the presence of something so strange that it would cause the little animal to behave in that way. Still shivering, she carried the cat downstairs.

'It was only when we reached the sitting room that her trembling eased,' said Grace.

However, the strangest event happened in the summer when she and her sister were alone in the house. Neither of them were fanciful people. Grace was 30 years of age at the time; her sister was 25 and she, too, had a very practical nature.

They had visitors arriving from America and their brothers had gone with their parents to Shannon to collect these relatives. To accommodate them, the two sisters had moved out of their room into the empty bedroom where their brothers used to sleep before they married. It was a huge room with two double beds and a large space in between.

In mid-August at about half-four or five in the morning, when there was just that slight bit of dawn light, Grace woke up with a sudden jerk when she heard the loud bang of the back hall door. She quickly sat up in bed, and then called to her sister across the room to wake her but she was already awake.

'There must be a burglar in the house,' she whispered.

The two of them listened, hardly breathing, and what followed was the most terrifying experience for them because what they dreaded was actually happening; someone or something with an extremely heavy tread began to move downstairs and along the passageway. Even though the hall was carpeted the footsteps were like those of someone determined to make its presence felt.

Whoever or whatever it was moved steadily along the hall but as Grace said, 'In your own house you know every creak

and we were able to follow those until whatever it was reached the bottom stair. It ascended the stairs with the exact same measured tread as before, until it reached the middle landing where there was a very creaky board.'

The sisters, much to their consternation, heard that creak very clearly. The disturbing sounds continued on up the next flight of stairs to their floor. They sounded so deliberate, like those of a huge man walking, that Grace realised she was holding her breath as the treads continued, steady and heavy, until they stopped right outside their door. Although there was a space underneath the door, there was no shadow of anyone showing in this space.

Grace said, 'I just could not describe the absolute, total terror that both of us felt at that time. Hearing that measured tread coming closer and closer, I felt as if I was suffocating.'

As she remembered her experience, I could see that she was still upset.

'We were sitting there in the beds, we couldn't move because there was nowhere to go. Where could we hide? Even if we'd wanted to move there just was nowhere,'

Grace went on. 'Because we were in a state of awful panic, it's hard to put a time on it, it could have been fifteen minutes or half an hour, we were just petrified, sitting there.' Her sister whispered in the darkness, 'We better search the house.' Grace didn't want to leave the safety of the room but her sister was a lot cooler. They hadn't heard any footsteps moving away from the door and nothing, absolutely nothing after they had stopped outside of the bedroom door!

So, because they were in their brothers' bedroom and both brothers were mad keen fishermen, there were gaffs, fishing nets and rods stacked in the corner. They took a weapon each: Grace chose a gaff, a pole with a big hook for lifting fish out of the water, and her sister a heavy rod. They inched the door open and with dry mouths and ragged breaths they looked out to the landing. It was completely empty.

'My sister headed off. I was tiptoeing behind her and we began to search the house. The clammy perspiration of fear was rolling off both of us but we searched around the window alcoves, checked that the windows themselves were locked, looked under every bed and in every wardrobe in every single room of the house. Nothing had been disturbed. The front and back doors were still locked and there was absolutely no sign of any entry.'

They crept back to bed, shivering and still scared.

When their parents came home, the sisters told them what had happened, but they said very little. The sisters suspected that their parents knew the house was haunted. A couple of years after their father died, Grace met his personal secretary in the town one day and during the conversation asked her if she knew anything about this. She just smiled at her and said nothing. Grace believes that she was being very loyal and honourable to her father. Grace was sure that her father must have asked her not to say anything to the children because it would have made them nervous.

'Still,' said Grace emphatically, 'there definitely was something there.'

Before that experience, Grace was sceptical of anything ghostly but said that no one could tell her now that there is no such thing. She and her sister talk quite

often about that experience, reliving it, tasting the terror.

'There were two of us who experienced this and we know that it happened. If I had been on my own I suppose that, looking back, I would wonder, but no, even if I'd been on my own I would still be certain that it happened. My sister, if she were here, would tell you exactly the same story. It happened and it was horrendous. Even thinking of it now, I shiver with the terror again. I live with it and sometimes I wake in the middle of the night and think, "My God! That experience!" I mean, in your own house you know every creak, every sound, and I still dread hearing that. But even though I am in a new house I still think of Balliniska as home and, in spite of its ghosts, I loved it.'

Another thing happened one time when Grace was away on holiday. Her nephew came up to stay with her father one night. He was to sleep in the other front bedroom and when he went upstairs he sat reading in bed but also had the television on. All of a sudden the bedroom lights began to go on and off, almost as if they were on a dimmer switch, but there was no such thing in the house. The lights went very gradually down until it became dark and then after a few minutes they came on again. It was in that same room that he and his cousin on another occasion saw a shape forming in the corner before it moved to the double bed at the other side of the huge room. On that occasion the 'thing' began to move and writhe in the bed but there was nobody there, just a shadow and the bedclothes moving.

One other time Grace's youngest brother was sleeping in the room where she and her sister had their terrifying experience. He awoke one morning at twilight and there was a man standing beside his bed. He was wearing a hat and as her brother looked at him the man just gradually began to fade until he completely disappeared.

Beechill County House Hotel

Patsy O'Kane and her brother now own Beechill Country House Hotel. After at least 350 years of exile, the O'Cahan clan finally came home.

The hotel has a well-deserved reputation and Patsy has played hostess to many eminent visitors. President Clinton and his wife Hillary stayed there, as did Lord Saville of Newdigate when he chaired the Bloody Sunday Inquiry.

The townland on which the house stands was and is still known as Ballyshaskey. Captain Manus O'Cahan asked Alexander Skipton to build him a house on this land, but by legal skulduggery Skipton took it from O'Cahan at the last moment, thereby beginning the saga of tragedy and ghostly appearances that dogged the owners down through the centuries.

Suffice it to say that Skipton never lived to enjoy the house. The night before he was due to move in he was killed by one of the O'Cahans. Three of the clan had entered Skipton's house at Tamneymore, and although their only intention was to find the deeds to the house to prove that Manus was the true owner, Alexander charged in and in the ensuing affray he was shot. He died instantly.

It was said that although he never lived there, his ghost haunted Ballyshaskey House, looking for his rightful place. But the restless spirits brought misfortune

Beech Hill County House, now a beautiful hotel in tranquil surroundings. The strange Revd Alexander is said to have haunted the building since 1793.

to Alexander's heirs because his son and heir, Thomas, scarcely escaped massacre when the house was burnt to the ground in the rebellion of 1642. A second house, Skipton Hall, was built in 1663 but the besieging Jacobean army burnt it down in 1688. Thomas's son, Captain Alex Skipton, built this third and present house in 1729. He gave it the name Beech Hill, on account of the number of beech trees then growing around it.

His son, also Alexander, was a strange man who often had unhealthily long conversations with the ghost of his grand-father. When he was a young blade and one of the 'gentry' set, he went through a mock marriage with Isabella Kennedy. It was just a prank but Alex fell madly in love with her and proposed. She accepted, but on the day that they were married they had an argument and in a fit of rage he went off to live in Benone. Isabella quite contentedly lived in Beech Hill, apart from her husband, for seven years. When he finally decided to return, she stood no nonsense and told him that it was his choice to live apart for the first seven years and now it was her choice to do the same. However, if history is to be believed, her words were harsher than her actions because they did manage to have a child, Thomas, who eventually lived at Beech Hill with his wife.

Although Alex and Isabella's marriage was a strange one, when she died before him he was heartbroken. She was the last of the Skiptons to be buried in the old cemetery; when Alex died in 1793, aged 80 years, he was the first of the family to be buried in the new cemetery of Glendermott. Perhaps Isabella had pre-viously requested not to lie with Alex in death or perhaps she had a supernatural hand in his internment in a completely different cemetery, even before it was consecrated. After all, what wife could tolerate being discarded on her wed-ding day and living alone for seven long years in a house, empty except for the servants?

Perhaps this is the reason for his haunt-ing; maybe he his ghost wanders around the grounds and the house looking for the wife whom he wronged on their wedding day. There have been many sightings around the area, particularly near the stream that runs by the house. The spectre of a figure, presumed to be Alexander, dressed in a swallow-tailed coat and top hat and sporting a clerical collar wanders around rather aimlessly, looking, it is believed, for forgiveness from his wife.

In the mid-1900s a house was built beside the old stables for Mr John McLaughlin, the land steward of the Ballyshaskey estate. Mr McLaughlin swore that the ghost of the Revd Alex haunted the house. He told of the figure passing him on the stairs and disappearing through the front door. Each sighting was accompanied by a distinct chilling of the air. Mr McLaughlin, hoping to dispel the ghost, had the house blessed by the parish priest.

One time, when John was in the big house presenting his accounts, the ghost came out of the drawing room and walked to what used to be the front door. John called out to it but the figure continued to move slowly. Eventually it faced him, and such was the malevolent expression on the face that a very fright-ened John lifted up his gun and fired it. The shot went right through the strange form and lodged in the architrave of the doorway. The figure disappeared.

The sightings continued in the stew-ard's own house and were verified in

1951 when two women stayed there on the night before the wedding of one of them. They both woke up during the night with a feeling of intense cold that quickly turned to fear when they saw an altar moving through the air towards them, while a figure of a man dressed in black and wearing a clerical collar hovered in the corner. This time the face was almost cavernous and the women screamed and fled from the room. Mr McLaughlin entered the room to see what could have frightened them and he was assailed by a terrible stench that seemed to emanate from the corner.

The next day, after the wedding, the parish priest, Fr McNicholl, performed a religious service and walked through every room in the house, blessing each with holy water. He walked down the road blessing it all the while and praying until he came to the bridge, where he stopped. He gave a last blessing and prayed aloud and those who looked on reported that the leaves swirled viciously around the priest until they disappeared beyond the bridge. Later Father McNicholl explained that he could bring the spirit no further but assured those who had experienced its malevolence that it had no power to return.

There have been no sightings since then, although people are reluctant to walk the road near the bridge at night.

The Three Ghosts of Belmont House

My introduction to Belmont House was in the early 1980s when I volunteered to work there one morning a week. My first thought when I looked at this beautiful mansion was that it was not what I expected to see in the suburbs of a town in Northern Ireland. My eyes travelled over its perfectly proportioned frontage and as its windows caught the light of the morning sun the whole house seemed to glow. It was difficult to believe that this beautiful mansion was haunted by at least three ghosts.

However beautiful this present house is, it is not the original Belmont House, the history of which can be traced back to 1696. The Lecky family from Scotland leased the land from the Irish Society in 1614. In 1696 Alexander and Alicia Lecky, having fallen in love with the city, commissioned the building of a mansion on the hill at Belmont on the site where the present house is today. They were unaware then that an ancient stone, known as the Crowning Stone of the clan of the O'Dochairtaigh, was in its grounds. There is some credence given to the hauntings when one considers that during the Plantation of Ulster the ancient clans and their lands were usurped to make way for the Planters. At night local people have attested to the fact that sounds like those of a battle have been heard near the stone and an effigy of a knight, now in the Tower Museum, was found in the grounds when the land was being excavated for the house to be built.

The Leckys chose the site because then it would have been surrounded by green fields and woods with a wonderful view of the city beyond. The Lecky family considered themselves to be very important in Londonderry. Indeed there was some foundation for their snobbery because in 1667 Captain Alexander Lecky was High Sheriff of Londonderry and served as Mayor in 1691 and 1695. Such was his importance in the town that the Lecky Road is named after the family.

Belmont House – the home of three ghosts: the Captain, the housekeeper and sad Mary.
(Courtesy of Maire Mullan)

'He took a considerable part in the siege of Londonderry, being captain of one of the six companies raised for the protection of the city; but on his refusal to accept the Test Act of 1704, he had to relinquish his office of alderman of the city and all his other offices.'

Some of the older people around would say that the ghostly figure of a tall man seen in the area known as 'The Planting' in the grounds of Belmont is probably that of Captain Lecky. A young boy called Billy Morrison, who, in the early 1960s, on a lovely spring morning took his dog out for a walk, gave an eyewitness account of this ghostly apparition. Although the Belmont grounds were private, Billy had no option but to follow his dog, which had run towards the wooded area. The dog was barking and whimpering near a fallen tree and what Billy saw when he approached made him stand rooted to the ground with fright. A tall man, dressed in a cloak and black felt hat, rose about 7 feet in the air, but Billy could see no features on the face

of this strange and frightening creature. The phantom figure hovered above Billy for some three minutes, but when the dog ran off, still barking, Billy followed. At the gateway he looked back and the figure had come closer. Billy screamed and ran as fast as his legs could carry him to his granny's house in nearby New Street. In a torrent of words he poured out what he had seen but she did not seem surprised. She sat him down and gave him a mug of hot sweet tea, simply remarking that the figure he saw was just 'The oul' captain'.

There are other stories about the captain, who was known to be a stickler for good manners. The housekeeper had a young son who was supposed to help in the gardens but was often seen running a bit wild. The captain's patience was running out, so he took his housekeeper to one side and told her that if she didn't keep her son under control then he would have to take steps to do so. The story handed down is that one day the boy went too far and the master lost his temper. He was heard to shout at the boy and threatened dire punishment. Shortly afterwards the young boy was found lying injured in the grounds. No one knew what had happened but when her son died a few days later the housekeeper blamed his death on the master. Her ghost sometimes can be heard crying during the night, according to one of the staff that was working there when it was a boarding school. The eerie figure has been seen on the stairs and on the corridor at the top of the back stairs to the servants' quarters. This apparition has also been seen at the front window of the drawing room, frantically beating on the glass and crying in silent anguish. After a few moments the figure fades.

The third ghost is that of a girl. The Lecky family lived in Belmont until at least 1820 when Thomas Lecky, a descendent, lost all of his money and may have sold the estate. It is believed that the

The housekeeper is often seen on the stairs of Belmont House.

original mansion was demolished and that about the year 1833 Mr William Millar, who came from Moneymore and was the collector of excise in the city of Londonderry, built the present Belmont House. According to a notice in one of the Londonderry newspapers, he died at his home in January 1834. All of his family are buried in the churchyard at St Columb's Cathedral, near the Courthouse wall, where the family gravestone can be seen.

But there is a mystery surrounding his daughter Mary, who, according to records, died just one year later at Belmont, aged 18 years. Even though Mary was said to have been a 'recalcitrant but lovable' child when she was younger, she was still the apple of her father's eye and when he died she fell into a deep depression from which she never recovered. Is the ghost of the young girl who has been seen wandering around the grounds and the house the ghost of Mary searching for her father?

In life she was no stranger to the servants' and kitchen quarters and despite her mother's orders not to mingle, Mary took little notice and seemed more comfortable with the servants than with the dignitaries who came to visit her father. She spent much of her time with the cook, to her mother's displeasure. When Mary went missing her mother knew that she would be found there, in the kitchen, listening to the gossip of the cook and the servants or following the servants around as they did their work. Often she hid from her parents and was even known to slip outside at night to meet with the children of the gardener. Was she still playing the same tricks in death as she did in life?

Later, the Macky family, who are listed in Burke's Landed Gentry of Ireland in 1837 as the 'Macky family of Belmont', owned

Belmont House. In 1860 Mr Macky was an agent for the Bank of Ireland. The Mackys had ownership of the house until the 1940s. They were very wealthy people and owned hundreds of acres in the area. The family knew of the ghostly reputation of the house but seemed to live alongside the ghostly residents very well, unlike the tenants who followed.

Records show that the house was rented to Sir Frederick Simmons in the 1930s. His family were not so laid back about the hauntings and had no desire to hear of any of the stories whispered by the servants. One of the maids refused to venture upstairs alone because she knew that 'someone was watching her'. She was asked to leave when she told of seeing a ghost of a tall woman, wearing a dark dress and bright apron 'floating' in the corridor leading to the servants' wing of the house. This ghost too has been seen on numerous occasions through the years.

During the Second World War, Belmont housed American Army personnel who were 'tickled pink', in the words of one officer, to be billeted in a haunted house, but after they left at the end of the war the house was divided into flats for several families, because at that time there was an acute housing shortage in the city. One family who lived in the sloping-ceilinged room, which was the servants' common room, told of coming in one morning and finding their daughter chatting to an unseen person. When questioned she answered, 'I was talking to Mary.'

The family left in a great hurry and moved into a cramped terraced house in the Glen area.

'I'd rather share a cramped house with the living than a big house with the dead,' was the mother's explanation.

In 1960 the Western Education Board bought the mansion and it opened as a boarding school for children with special needs in 1961. During the time when boarders lived there some teachers and the matron lived in. The duty teacher one evening walked along the downstairs corridor, immediately below the servants' corridor, and almost fainted when she saw an apparition of a very tall woman, dressed all in black, cross the passageway in front of her. The strange thing was that there were no doors at that particular point and the figure seemed to simply float through the wall on either side.

There is an impressive staircase with wrought-iron bannisters running from the wide hallway to the old ballroom upstairs. A man wearing a long black coat and carrying a tall hat has appeared on several occasions near the old ballroom or on the stairs. A cook saw him some years ago at the top of the stairs. On another occasion when two of the kitchen workers stayed after school to decorate the canteen (the original breakfast room) for Halloween, they had the strange sensation that they were being watched. When they looked towards the door, which is just behind the staircase, they both saw the figure. He was wearing a hat this time but his features were indistinct. The two women fled into the kitchen and several moments later when they peeped out the figure was gone. About three days later the cook saw the same figure in exactly the same place. Was this the captain checking up on those working in the house?

The school secretary, Denise, said that she had seen a ghost in the hallway near the canteen and on another afternoon, just after school hours, when she was walking down the corridor towards the back of the house, a black figure seemed to swoop from one side to the other and fade as it disappeared before her eyes into the wall. The only doorway on that side was the one to a small room that was used as an office and was originally the gunroom, and another doorway was at the bottom of four steps leading into the 'coal hole'. This door was always locked even in the earlier days of the household. Denise said that she was not frightened at the time but she wouldn't welcome that experience again.

There is talk that the mansion will be demolished to make way for a new amalgamated school on the site. It would be a pity if such a historic building was to be destroyed and one might wonder what would happen if the ghosts were left without a home. Would they congregate around the interesting antiquities in the garden, such as the Crowning Stone of the O'Doherty Clan, or indeed would a new broom also sweep that away?

The Ghosts that Haunt Boom Hall

No book on Derry hauntings would be complete without a mention of Boom Hall. Although it is now a ruin, I was invited to visit it by the last person to reside there, Miss McDevitt. She was an English and Latin teacher at Thornhill College, then known as the Convent of Mercy Grammar School, Thornhill. When I returned to teach in the school in the 1970s, Miss McDevitt, although retired, was often called upon as a substitute teacher. In the mornings she caught the school bus, since it passed the gateway to Boom Hall. In the afternoons I usually gave her a lift home and was invited in to have a cup of tea. Because I had heard

that Boom Hall was haunted I initially refused, but later, after some persuasion, I did accept out of politeness.

My initial impression was that it had a very gloomy interior with several rooms off the square entrance hall. The wide staircase on the left leading to the first floor was partially in shadow and dust motes floated in the light rays from the landing window. The dark wooden bannisters cast warped shadows on the flagstones covering the hall. Miss McDevitt lived mainly in what she called the morning room, which looked out over the river. The room must have been beautiful in its day with the high ceilings, the ornate cornices and chandelier, but at that time it looked weary for the want of necessary maintenance and a heavily carved sideboard dominated it. She admitted that she had neither the will nor the means for the upkeep that the house needed. I did not stay too long on the occasions when I accepted her invitation. Every time the hall echoed to the

The front of the now deserted and derelict Boom Hall, said to house the ghosts of Mrs Alexander, her grandson Waller and a young English relative.

sound of our footsteps I almost prepared myself for the ghostly appearances for which the house was famed.

In Colby's book, *Ordnance Survey of the County of Londonderry* (1837), Boom Hall is described as a fine example of a classical villa and it has an illustrious history. In 1779, ninety years after Derry was saved from the starvation of the Great Siege of 1689, Boom Hall was built by John Alexander, younger brother of the first Lord Caledon, on the west bank of the River Foyle. The site is of great historical importance because it was there that King James established his headquarters during the siege and it was from there the famous wooden 'boom' was erected across the river to prevent help from reaching the besieged city.

It was a formidable obstacle, which defeated many onslaughts until three ships, *The Mountjoy*, *The Jerusalem* and *The Phoenix* succeeded in breaking it. There was a delirious welcome for the ships' crews when they landed at Shipquay to unload their cargo of food. Unfortunately, Captain Robert Browning of *The Mountjoy* died of wounds received in the battle to relieve the city.

The land surrounding Boom Hall was known as Gunsland and was also the location of Charles Fort, which played a part

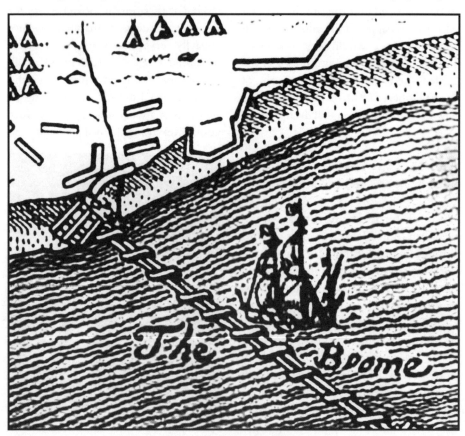

The wooden boom that was erected across the River Foyle by the Jacobean forces as part of the Siege of Londonderry. It held the city under siege from 10 June 1688 until 1 August 1689 when The Mountjoy finally broke through to relieve the city.

in the siege of 1659 as well as the later Great Siege. Skeletal remains, believed to be of soldiers and citizens who died during the sieges, were found in the area nearest the road when the foundations of a new church, St Peter's Church of Ireland, were being dug.

All of this history adds to the reputation of Boom Hall and its lands being one of the most haunted parts of the city. Stories abound of ghostly visitations, one of which is supposed to be the spirit of Captain Browning. It is said that his wife Jane watched from the shore, from the site of Charles Fort, believing that she would see her husband soon, but it was not to be. Could it be that it really is his ghost that is reputed to walk along the river on the land known as Gunsland in search of his wife, to fulfil a promise that he would return? There have been stories that on misty evenings sounds have echoed across the water and a tall man stands perfectly still, looking towards the river before moving in an erratic way along the riverbank. Some say he wears a military garb but no one really knows. The secret lies with Captain Browning in the churchyard of St Columb's Cathedral.

The house was handed down through John Alexander's grandson Robert to his son Henry, a diplomat who eventually died in South Africa in 1818. The estate then passed to Lord Caledon, a distant relative who sold it in 1849 to Daniel Baird, a wealthy merchant of the city, for £6,000. Because of the many changes of ownership it is difficult to pinpoint who the spectres that haunt it may be.

One story involved a girl who was a relative of the family. She had been sent to stay with the Alexanders in an effort to remove her from the attention of a young groomsman employed in her own home in England. Love being what it is, the young man followed her and hid out in the stables where they had secret trysts. When they were discovered, the girl was locked in an upstairs bedroom and the young man was banished. The girl pined and a few weeks later there was a fire in the bedroom. The family frantically fought the flames, terrified that the young girl under their protection would die such a horrific death, but eventually when the flames were extinguished the body of the young girl was not to be found. Perhaps she did die or more likely she made her escape to follow the young man. Some years ago a group of people were visiting the ruined hall, and they were adamant that in the gloom of the late afternoon a shimmering form of a young woman appeared at the aperture where a top window once was.

The Alexanders were important people in the city. William Alexander (1824–1911), was Bishop of Derry and later Primate of Ireland; his wife Cecil Frances Alexander wrote the hymn 'All Things Bright and Beautiful'; and Field-Marshal Harold Alexander (1891–1969) was renowned for his bravery during the Second World War and later became Governor General of Canada.

Over the years, the house was let to several people. The last occupier was Michael Henry McDevitt who owned a haberdashery business in Derry and had leased the house from Mr Maturin-Baird. However, during the war the Royal Navy requisitioned it and the WRNS who were billeted there apparently left it in a dreadful state.

After the war in 1947 McDevitt approached the owner, who was delighted to sell it, and there was some local talk that the ghostly residents were responsible for the price being lowered. He even offered to do the extensive repairs needed. The sale went through in 1947 and the McDevitt family moved back in.

Miss McDevitt, the last owner, must have led a lonely life in that mausoleum of a house. Even on a bright summer's day it had an eerie sepulchral feel about it, although she was quite proud of its history and when asked had no hesitation about sharing it. I asked her about its reputation as a haunted house. Her answer was quite straightforward,

'Of course it is. They keep me company. There's no need to fear the dead. It's the living that will do you harm.' That is a phrase I've heard often since I started gathering stories of ghostly goings-on.

She was proved right because the house was burgled several times and valuable items of silver and even furniture were taken. Obviously the thieves had no fear of ghosts either.

A well-known local historian, Ken McCormack, tells of an even stranger story that came to light when William Alexander's anecdotal notes were discovered. According to these notes, Martha Waller married Sir Robert Alexander in 1793. They had four children; the youngest, Waller, was born in 1796, just a year after his brother Robert. The two boys had the freedom of the extensive grounds of Boom Hall and often played in the front area. When he was eight he visited his grandparents in Drogheda and his parents were delighted to hear that he was enjoying himself immensely. Some weeks into his visit, his paternal grandmother, Anne Alexander, who lived with her son's family in Boom Hall, was descending the stairs and happened to look out of the window. Waller was playing and running around the front lawn. Anne rushed downstairs to see him, delightedly calling to Martha about how happy she was to have

Waller back home. Martha looked at her strangely and answered that Waller was still in Drogheda. The old lady decided to say nothing more but had a very uneasy feeling about what she had seen.

Two days later the terrible news arrived that Waller had suddenly been taken ill and died at the exact same time when old Mrs Alexander had seen him playing on the front lawn of Boom Hall.

There are other stories told of spirits haunting Boom Hall, its grounds and stables. Perhaps they are the spirits of the families who lived there previously: James, the 3rd Earl of Caledon, Thomas Bunbury Gough, the Dean of Derry, Daniel Baird and his wife Barbara, the Cooke family, and the Maturin-Bairds. Every family has its secrets, and some only emerge after death, so beware when walking on haunted grounds.

Further Stories of Hauntings in and around Boom Hall

Stories of the hauntings of Boom Hall did not stop at the big house itself. Ghosts were known to haunt the estate, the driveway and the gate lodge. The McCarron family who lived in the gate lodge of Boom Hall often saw a 'white lady' who simply stood at the gates, looking back towards the big house. They would pass by and followed their mother's advice to 'look to the right and take no notice' because it was a regular occurrence, and even the fact that no one else saw her didn't faze them.

When the family were younger, a cousin, Jim, used to visit, and on one occasion when they were all in the living room to the right of the hallway, playing some silly card game, he heard the front door opening and then closing with a very loud bang. He looked around, expecting someone to enter the living room but the footsteps passed and then he heard the back door slamming.

'Who was that?' he asked.

'Pay no attention,' he was told, 'it's just the ghost.'

'But I heard another door slam and you don't even have a back door! Where did it go?'

'Don't know,' was the answer, 'but there was supposed to be a back door there before the hall was made into a room.'

'There were other stories too about Boom Hall,' said Jim. 'For a time there were a couple of flats in the house and Madame Bec, the milliner, rented one of these. I remember that because when I served my time as a joiner, I was sent there to do some maintenance work. She told me that she'd seen a spirit or ghost of an old lady standing on the landing looking out. Madame Bec also mentioned that she had seen a pale form of a woman standing beside the gate lodge and that she had swerved to avoid her, only for the figure to disappear.'

Perhaps this was the ghost of old Mrs Alexander who had stood at the landing window and watched the spirit of her grandson playing in the garden.

Jim went on to say that his Uncle Paddy McCarron had the stables and he ran a riding school from there. Apparently, during the Second World War, when WRNS were housed in Boom Hall, there were times when he answered a knock at his door only to be faced by very frightened girls who had fled from Boom Hall and come running to the gate lodge, screaming because they had seen a ghost. Jim's uncle used to have to walk back down the drive with them. At that time there were trees and shrubs lining the drive

so Paddy said that they must have been in a very shocked state to venture up that lonely driveway in the dark. When they reached Boom Hall they always insisted that he come into the house and search it from end to end but with particular attention to the second floor.

When he escorted two of them back one late autumn night after one such incident, the rest of the WRNS were huddled in one room downstairs, too terrified to venture upstairs. He tried to reassure them that there was nothing to be afraid of, although he himself knew from his own 'run-ins with ghosts', as he called them, that the house was haunted.

Before he left that night, one of

The ghost of Lady Jane, wife of Robert Browning, captain of The Mountjoy, who was killed on his ship during the Siege of Derry, is said to stand beneath this oak tree, waiting for her husband.

the WRNS broke into tears and said that when she was coming home to Boom Hall from the barracks the previous week she saw 'a woman dressed all in grey standing at the big oak tree, looking in the direction of the river'. The girl confessed that the figure seemed to be holding onto the tree for support and there was an air of complete sadness around her, so much so that she herself felt it. (As it happens there is an oak about 450 years old in the grounds of Boom Hall, and that is supposed to be where Captain Browning's wife, Lady Jane, stood when she heard of her husband's death on board *The Mountjoy*.)

Henry, the Ghost of the Old Mansion

On the outskirts of Derry there is a mansion, built for The Honourable The Irish Society in 1849. It was rumoured to be haunted by a manservant, but when a blessing was administered in the late 1970s the spirit was laid to rest.

The manservant was a grim, bearded figure called Mr Henry. The story is told that Henry was not a good sleeper and sometimes walked around the house at night. Often he was to be seen prowling the grounds as well when he had a particularly restless night.

Poachers and burglars sometimes climbed the high gate and Mr Henry was responsible for several of them being caught and subsequently imprisoned. He was apparently paid a handsome sum for his endeavours so he continued to be on the lookout for prowlers. According to the staff he hid behind bushes and scared the intruders by leaping at them from behind.

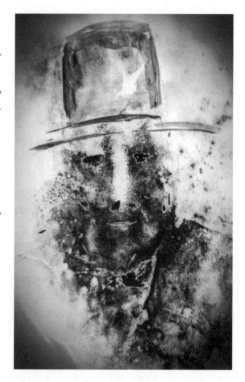

Henry, the long-dead manservant reputedly haunted an old mansion on the outskirts of Derry

In due course he passed away but there were mutterings among the servants and stories began to circulate that his ghost was to be seen lurking behind the shrubbery. His appearances did not confine themselves to the garden. It is said that his spirit was seen prowling the corridors, particularly the one at the top of the house, off which were the upstairs attic bedrooms where the maids slept. Some people suggested that in life he had more than a passing interest in the younger maids and often he was reported to the master for his unseemly behaviour. So one must ask whether in death his interest in young women survived.

The ghost of Henry usually appeared at the dead of night wearing his tall hat and staring with a fixed expression at anyone who was unlucky enough to encounter him. One maid was so terrified that she ran shrieking from her room but in her panic she tumbled down the stairs and seriously injured herself. Unable to work, she had to leave her employment and the rest of the servants mourned her death less than a year later. To the dismay and consternation of the few servants who remained, on several occasions the ghost of the young maid appeared on the stairs, wringing her hands and wailing. After 1924 this apparition was never seen again.

The stories of Henry were well known when the new incumbents moved in at a time of great upheaval in Derry. Several incidents of nocturnal disturbances are recounted but the owners of the house felt no sense of foreboding. As far as the residents were concerned, they were there to stay and if the house had to be shared by the spirits of the next world then so be it.

However, after a few years a new position was offered to the owners and they had to move away. Before they left the disturbances became very marked and they finally decided that a blessing was required. They asked a caretaker to remain and to arrange for the blessing of the house.

Two days before the priest was due to come, the caretaker heard a commotion upstairs. He knew that the house was empty except for him but there was no mistaking the sounds of furniture being dragged across the floor of the attic bedroom that used to be Mr Henry's.

He stood in the breakfast room, rooted to the spot, trying to decide whether or not he should vacate the house before the priest's visit, and then he heard a summoning bell ring in the kitchen. The kitchen door opened and the heavy footsteps of a man walked the length of the hallway and ascended the stairs. The caretaker rushed to the door but there wasn't a solitary soul there.

He stood listening and then tiptoed upstairs. When he came to the first-floor landing he heard the sound of drawers being opened roughly.

'I don't know where I got the courage, but my heart was pounding and I flung open the door but the room was completely empty. The wardrobe door stood open.'

He felt a chill creep into the room and then sweep around him like currents of icy air, and with a loud bang the wardrobe door slammed shut. When he turned he was looking at the image of himself in the wardrobe mirror.

'I was standing there looking at my reflection in that mirror when I saw this weird dark mist beginning to gather itself behind my image. I thought it was going to choke me because I felt the very air beginning to be sucked out of my lungs! I didn't look around but I got the hell out of that room and locked the door.'

When he went back to the kitchen he heard the little summoning bell. Looking at the line of bells he realised that it was the one to the room he had just left. The more he ignored it the more frantic the rings. He phoned the priest and asked him to come right away, which he did. He blessed the house and immediately afterwards the caretaker took his case and left with the priest, locking the door behind him. It crossed his mind that Mr Henry may have been back in that room, packing to leave the empty house too.

No sightings have been made since the 1980s. Perhaps the taciturn Henry realised that he was no longer welcome in a happy house.

Prehen House – The Tragic Tale of Mary Anne

How terrifying would it be to close the door of an old-fashioned bedroom, to slide in beneath the sheets only to feel the mattress sink down beside you and the coldness creep towards you? This might happen if you were foolhardy enough to spend a night in the haunted room of Prehen, for the ghost of John McNaughton is said to like the comfort of the room in which he slept when he visited the Knox family in 1745. So much does he claim it, that he is prepared to oust any visitors. Perhaps the ghost of the young Mary Anne hiding in the shadows or her ghostly presence hovering over the bed would assuage your panic. Perhaps not!

The first time I saw Knox's coach it intrigued me. It was housed in the museum in Gwyn's Institution in Brooke Park. The building itself was a crumbling forbidding edifice and lived up to the word 'institution'. The smell of mildew and dampness of the air inside made it an unpleasant building to visit. It was a fitting place for a coach in which a young girl was murdered. The coach was dusty and unkempt and the wheels still seemed to bear the mud of its last journey. It resembled the funeral coaches I'd seen in photographs, and the tragic, macabre story of the murder of Mary Anne Knox made the resemblance a reality. It is a story that haunted the city in the late eighteenth century and it continues to haunt it today.

Andrew Knox, father of 15-year-old Mary Ann, owned Prehen House and the wooded estate along the River Foyle in the Waterside. He was a Member of Parliament for a Donegal Constituency in the Parliament in Dublin. He was a very wealthy and influential man but his daughter was a wealthy young woman in her own right, having inherited a considerable fortune of £6,000. She also had the possibility of a further legacy of £1,500 each year if her 18-year-old brother George died without issue.

Prehen House was owned by the Knox family between 1740 and 1914. The ghost of 15-year-old Mary Ann, tragically killed by John McNaughton, haunts this house. John, or Half-hanged McNaughton as he is known, haunts the woods and house. (Courtesy of Colin Knox)

John McNaughton, on the other hand, was penniless, having frittered away the fortunes of the sizable estate of Benvarden. He was addicted to the frivolous lifestyle of the Anglo-Irish ascendancy in Dublin and in particular to gambling. He ran up enormous gaming debts and by 1750 was threatened with arrest for non-payment.

McNaughton had been friendly with Andrew Knox in their younger days and set out to renew their friendship by introducing him to some influential people who would be useful in his parliamentary career. In return, Knox invited him to stay in Prehen House until his situation changed. Honoria, Andrew's wife, made him welcome and introduced him to her son and daughter, unaware of his nefarious intentions. McNaughton was apparently aware of Mary Ann's inheritance and this was as much an enticement as her beauty.

Over time, McNaughton charmed the family, entertaining them each evening with music and card tricks. During the day he went out of his way to fraternise with the servants and gardeners. He succeeded in sweeping the young girl off her feet and had high hopes that her wealth would solve his financial difficulties. When McNaughton asked her father for her hand, Andrew refused outright having learnt that his so-called friend had embezzled money when he was an inspector of taxes. McNaughton was told to leave Prehen House and in a fury with his dismissal the scoundrel thought up a new plan of action.

He was, by now, desperate for money and decided that he would kidnap Mary Ann, marry her in a 'fake' marriage ceremony and confront her father with a *fait accompli*.

In the house of one of his friends he persuaded Mary Ann to read through a marriage service with him and one of his cronies acted the part of a witness. Although Mary Ann insisted that she would not go through a formal marriage without her father's consent and presence, McNaughton was adamant that they were legally married. Mary Ann, on her return to Prehen House, did not reveal what had taken place to her father.

It would appear that, in the following days, John McNaughton became more forceful and when Mary Ann realised the enormity of what she had done she confessed what had taken place. Andrew and Honoria Knox decided that Mary Ann should be removed from Prehen House for her own safety. Initially she went to Dunfanaghy and then to Sligo, but McNaughton followed her there, intending to abduct her. She returned to Derry but was unaware that some of the servants were keeping McNaughton informed and that he intended to carry out the abduction.

The opportunity came on 10 November 1761 when Andrew Knox decided to take his family to Dublin for the annual opening of Parliament and John McNaughton carefully laid his plans. A footman in the house was persuaded to sabotage the weapons of the travelling party, all except David McCullagh's which was beside him. Three men rode ahead on horseback, little knowing that McNaughton and three others lay in wait. When the first group passed, the ambushers prepared for the coach's arrival. It shook and swayed over the narrow rutted road, and when the masked figures burst from the bushes, shots ensued. Unfortunately Andrew Knox's blunderbuss failed to fire and McNaughton made his way round to the side of the coach and shot through the door, thinking that Andrew Knox was sitting in his usual place. But he wasn't and instead Mary Ann was mortally wounded, receiving five gunshot wounds. She died in agony some four hours later.

In the aftermath, troopers scoured the countryside and searched every dwelling looking for McNaughton, who had taken refuge in the hayloft of a Mr Winsley in Sandville, near Prehen. He was caught and brought to trial in Lifford. He never once expressed remorse for the terrible deed of murder and while he awaited his trial Mary Ann was laid to rest in the family plot in Rathmullan.

McNaughton presented his own defence at his trial and gradually sank into threats and insults so that further defence was refused. He was found guilty and sentenced to death by hanging, even though he claimed that he had no intention of harming his 'wife'.

Some people in the court were reduced to tears and the verdict was generally not a popular one: such was the sympathy for McNaughton that the executioner had to be imported from the Midlands. There are also stories that the gallows were constructed by men sympathetic to the prisoner, so they were not well made and when the trap was sprung the rope broke and McNaughton fell to the ground. The crowd called for his release and fought with the militia who were guarding the proceedings, but the prisoner got to his feet and declared in a loud voice that the hangman should do his work properly because he did not wish to go down in history as 'Half-hanged McNaughton'.

The next attempt was successful, and in the custom of that time, when the body had finished its death throes, it was cut down, beheaded and buried in Strabane.

However, for the people of the city, the story does not end there. There are tales of ghostly manifestations in the woods of Prehen, where the figure of John McNaughton is said to roam, waiting for Mary Ann to come to him.

There is a local song about McNaughton; the following is the first verse:

Deep are the woods of wild Prehen
There a ghost strikes fear in men,
Half-Stalks McNaughton, the Raparee
They hanged him high on the gallows tree.

In the house, it is poignant to read Mary Ann's birth inscribed in the Knox family bible: 'Mary Ann Knox, born November 13th 1741'.

Although crows fly and swoop over the woods of Prehen (in Gaelic *Preachain* means crow, after which the house is named), legend has it that when Mary Ann breathed her last, the crows that used to roost on the roof flew away and in the evenings the mourning coos of the doves that took their place can be heard.

It is said that Emily Brontë, in her only novel *Wuthering Heights*, quite possibly took her inspiration from the gruesome story of the murder of young Mary Ann Knox by John 'Half-hanged' McNaughton.

Springhill House and the Haunted Blue Room

When 'Good-Will' Coyningham married 16-year-old Ann Upton in 1680, her father was determined to look after her interests. In a marriage contract he demanded that the bridegroom should build a large house to keep her in the style to which she was accustomed.

Springhill House is beautiful; set as it is in the idyllic wooded surroundings of the countryside near Moneymore in County

Springhill House, where the tragic story of Olivia and George Coyningham is re-enacted by the ghost of Olivia. (Courtesy of the National Trust)

Derry. It is an impressive two-storied, tall-roofed house with a one-storey wing at each side. These were probably added on by subsequent generations of the Coyningham family. There are thirteen narrow windows in the main frontage and one might speculate that the unlucky number was connected to the tragic happening in 1814, some generations later.

> *My Dearest,*
> *Come home immediately. Your children have smallpox and I fear they will not live to see you again.*
> *Your loving wife,*
> *Olivia.*

Little did Olivia Lennox-Coyningham know that, when she hurriedly sent this letter to her husband, she would set in train a tragic series of events that would end in his death and the future hauntings of Springhill House.

When Colonel George Lennox-Coyningham received the letter from Olivia, he immediately set off on horseback to Springhill House. In his haste he neglected to tell anyone that he was going home nor indeed did he seek permission to do so. His children were dying and his presence at their bedside was paramount in his mind.

On the way, he met his good friend and commanding officer Robert Stewart and told him his reasons for rushing home to Springhill. Stewart raised no objections and bade him Godspeed.

When he reached home he was overwhelmed with relief to find that the children were recovering, thanks to the nursing care of Olivia. His relief was short lived however, because Stewart had reported him for abandoning his post and he was to be court-martialled for the offence. Lennox-Coyningham was shocked that his friend could do such a thing since he had covered for Stewart on other occasions. He was distraught at the betrayal, and to avoid the disgrace he resigned his post. Shortly afterwards one of his daughters died very suddenly and George sank into a deep depression that worsened during the following two years.

One night he went downstairs to the gunroom, took a pistol from the wall, returned to the blue room and entered the small dressing room beyond it. He sat on the chair, put bullets into the pistol and raised it to his head.

Olivia, having investigated the movements downstairs and finding the gun cupboard open and a gun missing, rushed to prevent his suicide. Breathless and filled with fear, she reached the door of the blue room whereupon she heard a shot coming from the small dressing room beyond. Rushing in, she saw that the door to the small room was partially open. Fearing the worst, she touched the door and when it swung open a little further she saw her husband slumped over the desk with blood from a head wound pooling over his papers. His gun lay on the floor, still smoking from the discharge. Beside it was the small bullet pouch.

Olivia screamed and servants came hurriedly into the room. They helped move George to the bed in the blue room and the doctor was summoned, but when he saw the nature of the wound that the colonel had inflicted upon himself he said that it was fatal.

George suffered greatly for two days before departing from this life. Olivia was broken-hearted. For days and weeks afterwards the servants watched her re-enact her rush to save her husband. They could only look on, helpless to comfort her.

Olivia later recorded the following poignant words in the family bible,

Captain Coyningham took his own life and his distraught wife Olivia haunts the Blue Room in Springhill House.

'George Lenox Coyningham, being of a melancholy mind for several months prior, put an end to his existence by a pistol shot. He lingered from 20th November 1816 to the 22nd, and died, thanks to almighty God, a truly penitent Christian …'

We would generally expect that the one who was driven to take his own life would be the ghost, but in this case it is not so. It is Olivia whose ghost still haunts Springhill House.

One can only imagine the horror and helplessness that she felt, knowing that she had arrived too late to save her husband. Perhaps this is the reason that her ghost has been seen standing outside the blue room door, her hands raised in horror and supplication, reliving the moments prior to her husband's suicide, knowing that she was only seconds away from preventing the tragedy.

In the late part of the 1880s a Miss Wilson came to visit and spent the evening chatting with Charlotte Lenox-Coyningham.

Feeling very tired, she excused herself and went to her room, the blue room. She was awakened by murmurings and noises and when she opened her eyes it seemed that the room was filled with alarmed servants. A door opened behind the bed and someone appeared and calmed the servants. When she woke in the morning she could see no door in the wall so believed that she'd simply had a bad dream. However, when, half-jokingly, she recounted the story to Charlotte Coyningham, she was told that there was indeed a door in that room, on the wall behind the bed, and that it had been bricked up and papered over many years ago to close off the room in which George had taken his life.

Although most sightings have been in and outside of the blue room, Olivia's ghost is not confined to that area. Her ghost has often been seen on the stairs floating swiftly towards the blue room.

In the twentieth century a nursemaid was returning to the nursery when she heard the children speaking to someone. By the tone and the content of their conversation she thought that an older person was in the room. She rushed in and saw Olivia standing over the children as if checking their wellbeing. The nursemaid felt no fear at all. Indeed she was moved by the concern that the apparition seemed to show towards the children. Within a few moments, evidently satisfied that all was well, the ghost simply faded away.

In more recent years, the blue room's wallpaper was stripped off and the secret door uncovered. It opened into a powder closet, on the floor of which lay an ancient pair of gloves and small pouch containing bullets.

In 1957 Captain William Lenox-Coyningham bequeathed Springhill House and its contents to the National Trust.

Ivy House

There is a strange ghostly connection between Captain William Coppin, his daughter Louisa and Sir John Franklin, the Arctic explorer. Louisa's ghost described the final ice-locked resting place of Franklin's expedition. Much is known about Sir John Franklin and his obsession to discover and traverse the last section of the Northwest Passage to be navigated, but in the city of Londonderry, which Coppin adopted as his own, few people know about the life of Captain Coppin.

The Coppin family lived in a tall Georgian house on the site where Tesco now stands. After William Coppin moved to Sackville Street, where he later died, the house had other tenants until eventually it was bought by the government, was renamed Ivy House and became the office for National Assistance in the city. Those who worked there speculated about some ghostly visitations and a strange blue light sometimes seen on the wall of one of the rooms.

Captain William Coppin was a man of great enterprise and invention. He was responsible for the success of shipbuilding in nineteenth-century Derry, but his interest began long before he came to that city. He was born in Kinsale, County Cork, on 9 October 1805, and despite his parents' warnings about exploring Kinsale's dockyard, one of the largest in the land, he often spent hours watching the men at work, building and repairing ships. Seeing the boy's interest, most were amenable to answering his questions and all of that only increased his fascination for the sea. When he wasn't at the dockyard he could be seen walking along the Cork coastline or on the banks of the River Shannon, no doubt dreaming of future adventures.

On one of these outings he saw a boat that had carried six Revenue men overturned on the river. Although he was only 15 at the time, he called for help, but realising that the men would drown before anyone could come he dived into the water and swam to the boat. He cajoled and encouraged the men to hang onto the upturned hull until rescuers arrived. For this spontaneous act he received a Bravery Award.

The world beyond Kinsale beckoned and he sailed for St John, New Brunswick and was soon employed at the shipyard there. He married Dorothea Smith, and a relative of hers, John Wilkins Smith, who owned a shipyard, pandered to William's higher ambitions and encouraged him to build his own boats in the shipyard.

William launched his first ship, *The Kathleen*, in 1829 and afterwards was commissioned to build *The Edward Reed* for a Derry timber merchant. He sailed it into Derry in 1830 and was enamoured by its wide river and the 'quaint' town. He readily accepted the command of a steam ship, *Queen Adelaide*, and later *The Robert Napier*. But not satisfied with that he pounced on the opportunity to buy the shipyard owned by Pitt Skipton of Beech Hill House.

He set up home in the lovely Georgian residence of Ivy House on the Strand Road so that he could 'watch as my ships took shape'. Captain William Coppin launched his first ship, *City of Derry*, in 1839 and the Londonderry Corporation presented him with an inscribed silver service.

His wife Dorothea settled in well and enjoyed the social life of the city. The Coppins were devoted to each other and Dorothea encouraged him to build his dream ship, *The Great Northern*. When it berthed at the East India Docks in

London it was described in the *Illustrated London News* as 'a remarkable monument of marine architecture'. However, Parliament reneged on its promise to purchase it for use in the Crimean War and eventually it was dismantled to pay London berth fees. It was a great blow for William, although he built other ships. His last one was named *Lady Franklin*. It was dedicated to the wife of the Arctic explorer Sir John Franklin who had set out in 1845, at the age of 59, on his fourth and last attempt to navigate the last uncharted part of the Northwest Passage. No word was heard from Franklin and his expedition, and after five years and several attempts to find the lost ships Lady Franklin was beginning to lose hope.

Meanwhile in Derry, in 1849, William and Dorothea's youngest daughter died just before her fifth birthday and they were devastated. They even continued to set a place at the dinner table for little 'Weasey' as the family affectionately called Louisa.

A few months after her death, her sister Anne and her other siblings reported seeing a strange flickering blue light moving across the bedroom wall. On occasion it seemed that the light even drew images and it indicated that it was the ghost of

The ill-fated exploration for the North-West Passage led by Sir John Franklin was lost. The three ships were presumed locked somewhere in the Arctic ice cap.

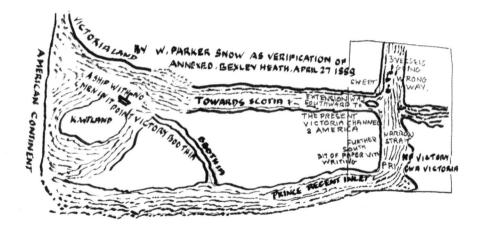

A copy of Louisa (Weasey) Coppin's ghostly chart of the location of Franklin's ship.

their little sister Weasey. Initially William did not give any credence to the stories, but when the light correctly predicted the death of the family's banker, he asked his children to put a question the answer to which the ghost of Weasey could not possibly know. Whatever had become of Sir John Franklin? The response astonished them when they watched a chart being drawn on the wall with the words, 'Erebus and Terror, Sir John Franklin, Lancaster Sound, Prince Regent Inlet, Point Victory, Victoria Channel.' The children reported this result to William when he returned home from his latest voyage.

He was still sceptical until he saw a second vision for himself. When Weasey was asked to describe the place, she answered with a vision of his ships in icy waters, along with a map and some letters upon the wall.

Mrs Coppin insisted that he should inform Lady Franklin of the vision and bring her a chart drawn by Weasey's sister Anne from the one that had appeared on the wall. They corresponded and Lady Franklin met with William on as many as thirty occasions, and it also appears that she may well have passed on some of the

advice apparently contained in these revelations to officers then preparing to leave for the Arctic to search for her husband.

MY DEAR MR COPPIN,
I have received your letter of yesterday, requesting me to tell you how far the 'mysterious revelations' of your child, in 1850, respecting the expedition of my late husband, correspond with the facts recently ascertained by Captain McClintock's researches.

In reply, I have no hesitation in telling you that the child's chart drawn by herself, without as you assure me having seen an Arctic chart before, represented the ships as being in a channel which we believed at that time to be inaccessible, but which it has since been found, they actually navigated.

Moreover, the names 'Victory' and 'Victoria', written by the little girl upon her chart, correspond with that of the point (Point Victory) on King William's Land, where the important record of the 'Erebus' and 'Terror' was found, and with that of the strait or channel (Victoria Strait) where the ships were finally lost.

I regret that I have not at hand your very interesting letter of May, 1850, in which you made to me those remarkable communications with more detail, but I believe I am quite correct in what I have stated. I have carefully preserved your letter and the child's drawing and you may be assured that they are in safety, and can be referred to, tho' it would be difficult for me to do so at this present moment.

Ever yours, dear Mr Coppin,
Most truly and obliged,
JANE FRANKLIN

Charles Forsyth and William Kennedy embarked on a search, but although they were closer than any other searchers for Sir John Franklin's party, they had to return, thwarted by the prevailing icy conditions. They did, however, discover the Bellot Strait, which had hitherto been unknown. Captain McClintock led a search in 1859 and discovered a note left on King William Island with the following words 'April 25; 1848, HM Ships Terror and Erebus were deserted on April 22, five leagues NWW of this, having been beset since September 12, 1846. The officers and crew consisting of 105 souls under command of Captain F R. M. Crozier landed here. Sir John Franklin died on June 11, 1847, and the total loss by deaths in the expedition has been, to this date, nine officers and 15 men.'

On the top right-hand corner were the words '... and start back tomorrow 26th for Back's Fish River'. That is the last that was heard of the expedition.

The BBC World News reported on 9 September 2014, 'Expedition sonar images from the waters of Victoria Strait, just off King William Island, clearly shows the wreckage of a ship on the ocean floor.'

Prime Minister of Canada Stephen Harper said in a statement, 'I am delighted to announce that this year's Victoria Strait expedition has solved one of Canada's greatest mysteries, with the discovery of one of the two ships belonging to the Franklin Expedition.'

The question remains unanswered as to how the ghost of a four-year-old child could possibly have given this documented information.

Sir William Coppin is buried in the churchyard of St Augustine's Church beside the Grand Parade on Derry's Walls.

The notation made by Captain William Coppin from instructions given by the ghost of his dead 4-year-old daughter 'Weasey'.

2

HOTEL SPIRITS

MANY hotels in Ireland were originally big houses belonging to the Anglo-Irish aristocracy. As such, they would have been the target of jealousy in life and revenge in death. Although some of the landlords would have been sympathetic, many saw their tenants starve and die during the Great Famine. It is said that these poor people returned to haunt the 'big house' that refused to help them. All over Ireland there are ruins of big houses, but of those that could be salvaged many are now hotels. However, it is believed that the ghosts of the tenants and servants still haunt them.

Bond's Hotel is now offices and a shop in Ferryquay Street Derry and is a lonely place at night. In the top room an unquiet spirit lodged.

The Ghost of Bond's Hotel

Near the foot of Carlisle Road in the city there was a smallish hostelry called Bond's Hotel in the early twentieth century. It was handy and inexpensive and was a decent place to stay for the artistes who appeared in the old Opera House next door. When it ceased to be a hotel in the 1960s it was turned into offices and Diana Stevenson opened a lovely bridal shop on the ground floor called 'Diana's the Bride'.

She told the following story to me.

When I first bought the shop I had heard tell of a ghost on the premises but I didn't think much about it. There were offices above the shop and I was made responsible for seeing that everyone had left and checking that everything was in order before I left the building.

35

One evening two or three days after I opened for business, I was closing up and by way of double-checking that all the lights were off, I looked up and saw that there was a light on in one of the offices on the top floor. I had thought that I was the last one left in the building so I went up the stairs to turn off the light.

I got a terrible shock when I reached the top corridor because there was a girl standing there, opposite one of the doorways. She was standing as if frozen and the thought that crossed my mind was that she was not well. She had pressed her back tightly against the wall and her whole body was stiff. Her arms and her hands were stretched out along the wall and she was oblivious to my approach. I didn't know the girl but I asked her if she was all right.

At first she didn't answer me and I asked her, 'Are you not well?'

'Oh', she cried out, 'I can't move. There's a presence here. I can't!'

'Don't be silly,' I said, moving forward. 'Of course you can. There's no one there.'

'Oh yes, there's a presence here. I can't.'

Just then a cold feeling of dread washed over me and I felt extremely frightened. It took me about half an hour to persuade her to move. I didn't want to leave her alone but I was certainly aware of something in front of us. The air was freezing even though the rest of the corridor was warm.

It seemed that the girl had some business with the office but when she arrived the office was closed. She had tried to turn the handle of the door and the lights in the office immediately turned on, and it was then that she felt the paralysing presence of someone or something.

I hadn't seen the girl beforehand and certainly not afterwards but I am convinced that there was a presence. I never ever went to that floor alone again.

The Ghost of Jones' Hotel

Jones' Hotel was one of the many hostelries in the city and was an obvious place for the esteemed writer William Makepeace Thackeray to stay. His observations took account of local folklore and gossip and in many cases he did not mince his words when describing the people that he met and the places in which he stayed.

In his *The Irish Sketch Book* he writes of his host.

He is a godly landlord, has bibles in the coffee room, the drawing room and every bedroom in the house, with this inscription—

UT MIGRATURUS HABITA
THE TRAVELLER'S TRUE REFUGE
JONES' HOTEL, LONDONDERRY

This pious or triple entendre, the reader will no doubt admire – the first simile establishing the resemblance between this life and the inn; the second allegory showing that the inn and the bible are both the traveller's refuge.

In life we are in death – the hotel in question is about as gay as a family vault: a severe figure of a landlord, in seedy black, is occasionally seen in the dark passages or on the creaking old stairs of the bleak inn. He does not bow to you – very few landlords in Ireland condescend to acknowledge their guests – he only warns you: – a silent solemn gentleman who looks to be something between a clergyman and a sexton – *ut migraturus habita!* The *migraturus* was a vast comfort in the clause.

It must however be said, for the consolation of future travellers, that when at evening, in the old lonely parlour of the inn, the great gaunt fireplace is filled with coals, two dreary funereal candles and sticks glimmering upon the old-fashioned round table, the rain pattering fiercely without, the wind roaring and thumping in the streets, this worthy gentleman can produce a pint of port wine for the use of his migratory guest, which causes the latter to be almost reconciled to the cemetery in which he is resting himself, and he finds himself, to his surprise, almost cheerful. There is a mouldy looking kitchen, too, which, strange to say, sends out an excellent comfortable dinner, so that the sensation of fear gradually wears off.

William Makepeace
Thackeray, *The Irish Sketchbook*, 1843

WILLIAM MAKEPEACE THACKERAY

William Makepeace Thackeray, who related the story of the Ghost of Jones Hotel.

The Seven-Year Haunting at the White Horse Inn

The idea of robbing people while they travel or stop at inns along their way is mentioned often in history. In the seventeenth, eighteenth and nineteenth centuries, trade and commerce were flourishing and there were subsequently many well-to-do travellers. Ireland was not a large country and there was still terrible poverty that drove men to rob those who had riches.

A coach ran from Derry to Newton Limavady, as it was known in the 1700s, and horses had to be changed every 20 miles or so, depending on how hard the driver drove them. The Campsie Inn (later named the White Horse Inn after a brand of whiskey that they sold) was in an ideal location to provide the facilities as a changing post, having stables at the back, some bedrooms upstairs and a warm welcoming meal on the table for the passengers.

The approach to the inn was by a narrow country road towards Broadbridge. In the dark days of winter this could be an eerie journey with the bare branches creaking and swaying above the coach. It was on such a night that the coach rumbled on the rutted road, and as the lightening struck blue in the black sky the coachman pulled his horses to a stop outside the inn.

What the passengers on the coach did not know was that two robbers, John McQuade and Robert Acheson, lay in wait inside the inn. They had seized the inn some time before and locked up the terrified staff. When the coach appeared they robbed and beat the passengers. Once they were finished divesting their victims of their money and effects they whipped the horses, sending them galloping away in a frenzied state. The robbers made their escape on stolen horses, leaving their victims bleeding at the entrance to the inn. One, Henry O'Hagan, died of his wounds.

But the outlawed robbers did not have it all their own way. They were later caught and the judge sentenced them to be hanged for the murder of O'Hagan. They escaped from Derry Jail while awaiting execution but were later recaptured and summarily put to death on the gallows in front of the jail in Bishop Street. Their bodies hung there for several days as a warning to others.

But that is not the end of the story. On a bleak November night in 1905, some men were playing cards in a room near the back of the inn when the gamblers heard the sound of horses' hooves thundering up the lane nearby. Disturbed by the unusual noise, they rushed to the window and saw four white horses pulling a coach and tearing towards the inn at great speed. The whole spectacle seemed to be enfolded in a luminescent light, so bright that the men shaded their eyes. The horses veered and sped around the back towards a small yard fronting an orchard. The seven men rushed outside and around to the rear but found absolutely nothing there. The yard was empty. It was the ghostly appearance of the unfortunate coach.

On another occasion in the late 1960s, 45-year-old George Cooke, a local Coolkeeragh power-station worker, had the frightening experience of seeing the coach come tearing out of the darkness

The White Horse Inn, still a place where people gather every seventh year to wait for the phantom coach to appear.

and clattering to a stop in front of the White Horse Inn. Mr Cooke said, 'Three passengers alighted from the coach and walked towards the inn. Then the sound of the coachman's horn rang out and with the driver lashing his whip over the backs of the four bay horses the coach thundered off into the darkness.' Mr Cooke was visibly shaken by the encounter.

In 1959, James McElwee decided to go for a drink to the White Horse Inn. He walked along the main road but was startled when he heard horses' hooves behind him. He jumped up onto the grass verge when he saw a coach and four brilliant white horses careering along the left side of the road. 'After passing me,' he later reported, 'the coach and horses drove around to the back of the inn where the old mail coach horse once watered and awaited its passengers. The driver was dressed in old-time clothing and was a stout friendly fellow. He got down from the coach and entered the inn. I followed him at a short distance but once inside I found no trace of him and no one in the pub knew what I was talking about. I looked outside and the horses and coach were gone.'

Whether or not it is just a local legend that the Phantom Coach will reappear every seven years the Cole family, who once owned the inn are adamant that they and their servants saw the coach and horses on several occasions, but unlikely as it seems, they did not see the appearance as something to be frightened of; rather, it was something that the people in the locality celebrated.

The next sighting will be in November, say the locals. Whether or not there is a manifestation, the legend will live on in local haunted folklore.

3

BAR SPIRITS

GHOSTS and bars seem to couple together quite well. The love of alcohol has been the curse of Ireland and many a mother was left without the money to put food into her children's mouths because of drink. Are the ghosts who haunt these bars the spirits of women who have been wronged?

The Argyle Arms Bar

The Argyle Bar on the corner of Argyle Street and Park Avenue was, and still is, a popular place for the local residents to gather. Some are sceptical of the word 'haunted' but many will not go alone upstairs from the bar.

Some years ago, a young man contacted me and spoke about an experience that his aunt, a resident of Argyle Street, had in the 1950s. Her house adjoined the Argyle Bar on the corner. At that time it was a small tavern, frequented only by the locals.

One evening she wanted to make a phone call but since phones were few and far between she went to the bar to make it. She left her young daughter in the house for the few moments that it took to make the call, but when she

Argyle Arms Bar is one of the many haunted bars in the city.

was returning she heard a child crying. Fearing that it was her child the woman hurried back to the house.

'I don't know what made me stop and look up at the window of the bedroom where my wee daughter slept. It was just something that came over me but I got the shock of my life when I saw, clear as day, an old woman standing there at the window above me, staring out. I went up those stairs two at a time but when I burst into the bedroom my daughter was lying in bed, staring at the window. There was no one else in the room.'

She lifted her daughter but the little girl kept pointing towards the window making frightened sounds and whimpering.

'Go away, go away,' she kept repeating but her mother couldn't see anyone.

When the woman's husband came home from work, the little girl told him about the 'witch' who was in the room. The mother added that she'd seen an old woman staring out but that she had disappeared by the time she got to the bedroom.

'I began to think it was my imagination,' she said, 'but I couldn't have seen her as clearly as I did. I know I didn't dream it.'

That night the little girl was restless and was still whimpering and talking in her sleep about the witch. Her mother brought her into bed with her but she too was unable to sleep.

'I was so afraid that if I closed my eyes the awful woman I saw would be standing beside me when I opened them,' she said.

Next morning the father asked a priest to come and bless the house. When the wife repeated what she had seen the priest put on his stole and went upstairs to the bedroom, sprinkling holy water and saying prayers as he went. He was in the room for some time and when he came downstairs he was shaking. Out of the hearing of the little girl he said to them, 'Take your daughter and leave the house straight away. There is something evil in that room.'

The man who related the story said, 'My aunt and uncle left that day and never went back, even to get their belongings.'

The owners of the bar bought that house. They extended the bottom floor into a lounge and converted the upstairs into toilets. There have been reports that the end toilets are haunted. They are where the little girl's bedroom would have been.

'I wouldn't go up there on my own,' said the nephew, 'would you?'

The Castle Bar

The Castle Bar nestles against the ancient Derry Walls at Castle Gate, one of the seven gates into the walled city. The bar was apparently owned by a sea captain during the nineteenth century and had a notorious reputation as a brothel.

There is an often-told story about the presence of a ghost in the uppermost storey of the bar, which has both fascinated and terrified the people who frequent it. The captain was a shrewd man who knew from his own seafaring days that sailors who had spent a long time sailing the oceans of the world needed some feminine company and relief when they came into port. So apart from looking after the thirst of the visiting sailors, the captain himself arranged for prostitutes to be available. It was a nefarious means of stripping the sailors of their hard-earned money. The rooms at the top of the building were made available for the prostitutes to carry on their business. Unfortunately, according to stories of the time, the girls themselves did not always have a say in the matter and many were abducted and forced into prostitution.

One such story records that a young girl was supposedly hired as a servant but, because of her beauty and youth, was locked in a room above the tavern. A drunken sailor who paid his dues unlocked the door and attempted to have his way with her. She tried to fight him, refusing to be used in such a way, but her calls for help went unheard and she began to scream. When the sailor could not quell her screams he hit her with a lamp, leaving her bleeding and badly injured. The captain's men rushed up from below and hurriedly hid her in a cupboard under the eaves before they spirited the sailor away and put him on a ship that was leaving port.

On their return they found the girl was dead and they placed her body under the floorboards of that room. When the prostitutes enquired about the girl they had heard screaming, they were fobbed off with the story that she had left with someone she knew. Needless to say, they did not believe the story and during the next months and years they were frightened by the strange unnerving sounds they heard coming from that room. So much so that they left one by one and the captain finally sold the tavern. One would hope that his conscience got the better of him but there is nothing in history to indicate that such a thing happened.

The new owner, on hearing the suspicions of the patrons of the tavern, investigated, and when the floorboards of the room on the top floor were lifted the grisly truth unfolded and the fate of the young girl was uncovered. The owner tried to discover the whereabouts of her family but was unsuccessful. He paid for a Christian burial for the girl but her ghost reputedly still haunts the top room.

Certainly the stories tell of an apparition of a young woman of about 15 years of age, dressed in the clothes of an earlier time, occasionally being seen; but more often it is simply her presence that is felt on the stairs and in the top room.

Castle Bar nestles into the City Walls and is steeped in history.

A barman who was working in the room several years ago said that a terrible chill almost froze his breath as it left his body and at the same time he heard the sound of heartbroken sighs. He said that he began to search around but that he had to stop when the room became so icy cold that he couldn't feel his hands. He began to blow on them to heat them up but they became icier and that was when he felt cold arms around his shoulders.

He ran from the room straight to the bar and drank a whiskey in one gulp. Even though the boss laughed at him, two other workers agreed that they too had experienced the same thing but were afraid of being thought foolish and fanciful. He left his job when he had a second similar experience, declaring, 'I feel sorry for the wee girl but I don't want to meet her ghost ever again.'

The Mourne Bar

The last owner of The Mourne Bar on Foyle Street was Danny Grant, who moved there when The Arch Bar in Bishop Street was demolished for the Fountain area redevelopment.

The Mourne became quite famous in the town because of the huge mural painted on the gable. It was of a love letter half inside an envelope. Danny was quite amused by this because Foyle Street was known as a 'street of ill repute' and the mural caused many a ribald remark to be made. People wondered if the mural was intended to symbolise the fact that many of the clientele in earlier times had been involved in loving pursuits!

However, shortly after the new owner moved in he discovered that there was a sinister atmosphere in the attic room. Strange sounds were heard, like those of a woman weeping and of chairs moving, but nothing in the known history of the building could explain the presence, for presence it certainly was.

There was a particular staircase on the way to the attic that seemed to house this presence and a previous owner told of an experience she had as she climbed it. She described it as 'a suffocating cold, clammy feeling, as if all the heat and oxygen had been sucked from the air.' She was unable to move upwards or downwards and a damp chill permeated her body for the few moments that she stood there.

After she came downstairs again she tried to convince herself that she had imagined it, but when it happened once again she knew that there was definitely something barring her way.

Later, an ex-barman with whom she had a chat told her that the same thing had happened to him, and he even began to believe that the ghost or spectre was lying in wait for him. That made him very afraid. In the end it was the reason he left.

When the area was targeted for development, Danny was quite happy to leave. Part of the new Foyleside Shopping Centre was built on the site but strange and fearful things have been known to happen during the construction and even since then. Night security workers in Foyleside have also experienced unusual things there on occasion, and more than one believe that the ghost has not gone away.

The Mourne Bar was demolished to make way for Debenhams but a presence has appeared in the middle floor of the shopping centre.

The Park Bar

The Park Bar is an old converted house at the top of Great James Street, one of the streets of Georgian houses that run from Francis Street and the Northland Road down to the Strand Road. There are two windows on the Francis Street corner of the bar. The lower one has stained glass and the upper smaller one is clear. It is at this small window that the spectre of a lady reputedly appears. No one seems to know how or why the spirit appears but when she does it is usually on a quiet and still evening.

The window faces St Eugene's Cathedral, which is diagonally across from the bar. One woman described the figure as a lady of middle years, dressed in very elegant clothes of muted colours fashionable in Georgian times.

An old lady who lived in the Lower Road was coming out of the cathedral after devotions one evening and happened to glance across and see the ghost. Not knowing the story, she was heard to

The Park Bar was once a family home near the top of Great James Street. One of the past residents, a sad lady, appears occasionally.

remark to her companion that the poor woman who lived in that house seemed very sad. She was left wondering why her friend rushed away in distress. When she spoke to her the following day she heard that the figure she saw was a ghost of a woman whose baby died in infancy and she died soon afterwards.

On another occasion two women were standing chatting at the cathedral gate and saw the woman appear, disappear and reappear every ten minutes or so until her face became just a pale blur. They did, however, report that the lady had a very melancholy expression. The two women went back into the church and prayed for her that she might rest in peace.

Rocking Chair Bar

The Rocking Chair Bar is at the top of Waterloo Street in Derry and a few years ago a woman who worked there was busy in the lounge on the middle floor, tidying up and setting tables for a function that evening. The lounge on this floor is on two levels, the second level being approached through a wide archway opposite the doorway. The woman had her back to the door, and when she heard it opening she glimpsed the dark shape of a man from the corner of her eye. She assumed that it was the waiter passing through. She continued to wash the tables and paid little heed to the heavy footsteps ascending the stairs to the top floor.

When she heard the heavy thuds and movement of furniture from above she smiled, thinking that she could ask him to check if there were any extra chairs and if so he could bring them down without her having to go up. When the sounds became very loud she began to think that

The Rocking Chair Bar.

there was more than one person on the top floor shifting the stuff so she called up for the chairs that she needed. She listened for a few moments but no one answered. Sighing, she went to the stairs called again. The sounds didn't stop, and feeling a bit exasperated she shouted above the din.

'I'm coming,' called the waiter from downstairs. She was shocked when he came to the bottom of the lower stairs.

'Who's upstairs,' she asked, 'I thought it was you.'

'Nobody,' was his answer. 'We're the only two here.'

Just then they both heard the sounds of something heavy being dragged across the floor. 'There's nothing up there that can be moved,' said the waiter, 'something's going on.' When he called out, 'Who's there?' the sounds stopped.

At that precise moment the woman saw something like a dark shadow slink past her and she shivered. An icy vapour clouded the air causing her to step back so quickly that she almost lost her footing on the top stair.

'Can you check upstairs?' she asked the waiter nervously, 'maybe somebody wandered in from the street.'

She waited at the central landing and the waiter went on up but when he came down a few minutes later he told her that no one was there and nothing was out of place. 'But it smells foul. You'd better clean it up.'

'No way,' she said, 'there's something weird going on and something passed me on the stairs. I'm heading back down. I'm not staying up here on my own.'

When they related their experience to other staff there was silence. Thinking that the others did not believe them, they were adamant that they heard and felt the presence of someone or something. No one disputed what they said.

When the same thing happened again a few days later the woman was terrified enough to leave work, vowing that she would never willingly enter the Rocking Chair Bar again.

The Sailor's Rest

The Sailor's Rest was usually very busy during the 'Scotch Fair', when those Derry and Donegal people who had left Ireland to work in Scotland returned home for their holidays. Before a rough journey on the *Laird's Loch* ship, Agnes Weston, the landlady and owner, provided a substantial breakfast for those patrons who stayed the night. At other times of the year, naval personnel took rooms there.

The bar was at the end of Foyle Street on the corner with Bridge Street. The building was formerly known as the Metropole Hotel (a new building called the Metropole now stands there) but the original building housed the offices of the Anchor Line passenger ships that traded with America.

It was said that the bar was well named for it was a respite for sailors whose ships came to berth at Derry Quay on the

River Foyle. Agnes's rules, one local man said, were a bit lax at times. That statement could be taken with a pinch of sea-salt coming from a local man who probably had a grudge against the glamour and attraction of the Navy men for Derry girls. The man added that this probably had something to do with the fact that the street was well known for being the haunt of 'women of the night'.

During the Second World War, while the Battle of the North Atlantic raged, allied sailors and personnel found relaxation and longed-for rest in Derry when they had some respite from their convoy duty. One of the places that provided these was The Sailor's Rest. Not only did it supply drink to soothe the fighting men but it also had some sleeping accommodation. For men used to the roll of the waves this was a delight.

In his memoir *War at Sea: A Canadian Seaman on the North Atlantic*, Frank Curry, recalled his first impression of Derry when he entered Lough Foyle after a particularly harrowing voyage: 'It was like a dream. It did much to restore our souls, even though we knew we would only have forty-eight hours layover. For those brief hours and days, we would become human beings again; in touch with peace and beauty and tranquillity; far removed from all the ugliness of war.'

However, all was not restful at the Sailor's Rest. At times, particularly when tides were high and rough and the river often reached the door of the Sailor's Rest, strange things happened.

One sailor from Ontario explained that he almost convinced himself that he was having a terrible dream, although he knew he was wide awake.

'I was on a ship and we were trying to outrun a U-boat. The captain ordered me to go to the boiler room to tell the men to get up more power but just after I got there I felt the horrendous jolt and crash of a torpedo and the boat began to take on water very quickly. The door to the boiler room was twisted and stuck and I couldn't get out. All around me men were screaming and all I could see were arms flailing. I was thrown amongst them, fighting for my life, but the strangest thing is this, I was aware that I was in both places at the one time. I was on board HMS *Drake* and yet, I was safe in bed in my own room in the Sailor's Rest.'

His was not the first experience of that strange phenomenon. Other men told the same story. Later he heard that the ship he saw in his vision, the HMS *Drake*, served in the First World War and was torpedoed by the German submarine U-79, commanded by Kapitänleutnant Otto Rohrbeck on 2 October 1917 in Rathlin Sound off the North Antrim coast. Eighteen men working in the boiler room were drowned.

'I still don't understand how this vision came to me. I could see and hear the captain giving his orders in German, a language that I don't speak, yet I understood him perfectly.'

NB: Recently, a small number of survivors of the convoys were presented with medals for bravery. The medals were earned at a terrible cost.

The Star Bar

The people who lived and worked in The Star Bar whispered stories of paranormal activities. Some of the stories that were repeated often told of seeing lights, hearing footsteps and even having people appear at the foot of their beds during the night.

There were several complaints made by people who heard loud noises like those that would be made by furniture being dragged or banged in the empty rooms above them. When the owner investigated he could find nothing to explain the disruptions.

The bar stood on the corner of Bridge Street and John Street, and during the 1950s it was known as The Canadian Hotel and was considered quite an elegant building for that part of town. The owners kept it beautifully maintained and its almost half-oval shape at the junction of the two busy streets was a welcome landmark for many returning emigrants.

It was often frequented by sailors from the many navies of Europe that sailed into Derry during and after the Second World War. There were British and Norwegian, French, Canadian, Spanish, American and Portuguese naval personnel aplenty.

In the 1960s new owners changed its name to The Star Bar and later it was renamed The Cutty Sark. It had quite a varied history, since at one stage it housed a funeral parlour and the undertakers kept the funeral horses on site. Men who frequented the bar before the building was bombed during the 'Troubles' in the mid-1970s remember seeing the arches for the haylofts within the original building. Perhaps the stories of ghostly appearances could be related to the business of undertaking.

Being quite close to the River Foyle, it was a handy stopover for people leaving or coming into the country by boat. It was close to the offices of the Burns and Laird Line whose boats sailed to Scotland, Haysham and Liverpool. During the years of high emigration it was a place where many tears were shed and promises made. For some people it was the last bed on which they slept in Ireland.

Some other disturbing stories repeated by people were of hearing loud noises such as those that would be made by furniture being dragged or banged in the empty rooms above them. When the owner investigated he could find nothing to explain the disruptions. He even locked the door to that room just in case someone was responsible for trying to frighten his customers.

But passers-by also told of lights like torchlight being shone down from the windows of the empty room. Thinking this to be a hoax, the owner planted someone outside who signalled when this occurred, but when he made a very hasty examination of the room he found that the door was still locked, and on opening it was clear that there was no one inside.

Perhaps the sounds that people heard and wraith forms that they saw were the echoes of those who had left these shores forever. One can ask if the strength of the longing and heartbreak of those poor people leaving materialised into their ghostly forms wishing to remain.

They may even be the spirits of those souls who were carried to the cemeteries in the black coach hearse from the premises long before.

We shall never really know and all of the happenings defied explanation.

4

HAUNTED HOUSES

WHO knows why a house is haunted? Usually the reason is embedded in its history – promises not kept, children not buried in consecrated ground, women wronged and mothers bereft of their children. Is it possible to give these unquiet spirits peace?

The Brown Lady of Elagh

When Anne was a young girl she went to visit her aunt who lived in a house near the Ness Woods in County Derry. It was an old and welcoming house but there was a mystery within.

A portrait of a woman hung in the sitting room and the people in the house referred to her as the 'Brown Lady' for the simple reason that the woman was dressed in dark-brown clothes against a sombre background in mottled shades of brown and black. Looking closely at the painting, one could see that although she was a young woman, she appeared to have a sad and subdued countenance. It was not a particularly attractive picture but it was part of the house for so long that no one ever thought to remove it from the wall.

When Anne asked about the woman in the portrait she seldom received a satisfactory answer, but as she grew older she realised that the people she questioned were always evasive. This just served to make her more curious and she badgered her aunt into telling her the real story behind the painting.

Each night the Brown Lady apparently left the picture and walked through the house, disappearing through the back door. Several times she was followed but her route never changed. She walked across the garden onto the road and did not stop until she came to Ardmore Cemetery. There she would stand outside the walls of the cemetery at a particular spot where she would appear to be in deep contemplation. After a certain time she would walk back to the house and disappear once again into the portrait. There was no malevolent feeling about the appearance and disappearance of the woman. Those in the house simply accepted it because this ritual had gone on as long as they had lived there.

A new priest came to the parish and heard some talk of the 'woman in brown'. He went to the house on a parish visit and the owners, at his request, told him

The dark image of the 'Brown Lady" that hung in a house in Elagh. She mysteriously left the painting each night.

After the grave of her baby was blessed the painting of the lady visibly brightened.

the story and showed him the portrait. He decided to check for himself if the story was true. That night he stayed on in the house till late.

To his astonishment, at the usual hour the priest saw the figure step from the portrait and walk through the house as the family had said. She showed no awareness of being watched as she walked along the road to stand beside the cemetery wall. He accompanied her back to the house but no word was uttered.

The next day he looked up the parish records and discovered that the spot on which she stood was the burial place of babies who had died before being baptised. In those days these areas were not consecrated. The priest prayed and meditated about the action he should take, and a few days later, with the permission of his bishop, he consecrated the graves of these innocent children.

That night he waited at the usual hour for the Brown Lady to appear. When she stopped to pray at that place a light transformed her face, she made the sign of the cross and with an ethereal lightness she glided back to the house.

Over the next few months the people of the house saw a subtle transformation happening before them. The portrait gradually became lighter and more serene. There was a sparkle in the Brown Lady's eyes and a glow of happiness surrounded the painting.

A doctor of the City of Derry told this story to me.

The Foyle Road Spirit

The River Foyle is wide and beautiful and has certainly earned its place in history. The famous siege of 1698–99 finally ended after 105 days when the boom across the river was breeched by *The Mountjoy*, a ship under the command of Captain Browning.

In the nineteenth century the city was thriving, served well as it was by the River Foyle. Alongside it were a shipbuilding business and docks from which people sailed to Scotland, England and further afield to America and Australia. Train lines ran along both sides of the river, moving people and merchandise to the east and west of the country. To facilitate the budding shirt industry there was a network of roads close to the river.

One such street was Mitchelburne Terrace, on the Foyle Road. This was a small row of houses named after Colonel John Mitchelburne who was made governor of the city during the siege in 1689 and later founded the first club of the Apprentice Boys in 1714. It faced directly onto the Foyle Road and on the opposite side the railway wall separated it from the river.

A woman who settled in England in the 1930s after her marriage to a Londoner owned one of the houses. Unwilling to sever her link with Derry she kept ownership of her house but rented it out. It had several tenants over the years but none stayed long. Whether or not she knew that the house was haunted, she kept her own counsel.

A young married couple who had lived with the wife's family for a few months after their marriage were delighted when they were told that they could rent the house. They couldn't believe that they had a house to themselves, unlike many other young married couples at that time; they redecorated it, bought new furniture and settled into married life.

The husband worked shifts and his wife was often alone in the house. At first she thought that the coldness she felt on the stairs and the uneasiness she often experienced were caused by her being in an old house in a strange area. Often, when her husband was working late, she slept on the sofa in the living room because she had a creepy sensation that when she went upstairs someone or some sinister presence was watching her. She kept her thoughts and feelings to herself, unwilling to appear foolish to her new husband and convincing

herself that it was just her imagination. When she did finally tell him he made light of it and refused to believe her story until one night he was alone in the house.

On that weekend she had gone to visit her sister in Donegal and at midnight her husband locked up and began to climb the stairs to their bedroom. When he was halfway up he had the same peculiar feeling that someone was staring at him and waiting for him on the landing. He ignored it and as he opened the door to their bedroom, two other doors crashed open. Suddenly he felt a gust of icy air circling around him starting from his feet and crawling upwards, leaving him unable to move. He began to pray and as he blessed himself there was an almighty crash in the return room and the door swung open. The wind whistled then raged through the house and even lifting the carpet on the stairs. As he prayed the wind died down and everything seemed to return to normal.

When he investigated the return room he found that a mirror that they had received as a wedding gift had fallen and smashed into smithereens.

'I was weak with fright,' he confessed later, 'and to tell you the truth, I went up to my sister's house and stayed there. I made the excuse that I'd forgotten my key.'

The next day when his wife came home he casually mentioned that the mirror had fallen off the wall. Not wanting to worry her he didn't say what had taken place beforehand, but when he saw her expression he realised that she knew something more sinister had happened. In the end, she coaxed the truth from him. Although in one way she was glad that she hadn't imagined those weird happenings, the reality was that something evil hovered around their home.

They resolved to have the house blessed and arranged for one of the local priests to come, but that night they had another visitation.

'I thought that whatever it was, it was warning us not to interfere. It happened around midnight, the same time as the previous night. Although the room was already dark we both saw a white, almost transparent shape hovering motionless at the foot of our bed. The room was so cold that we were shivering, even though we had plenty of blankets on the bed. The air just became colder and colder and I wanted to get up and confront whatever it was. I wasn't feeling brave or anything but my wife held onto me and begged me not to move. After what could have been an hour but was really just a few minutes it faded and the room became warmer.'

Neither of them could settle that night and that was the last night they ever slept in that house. They stayed with her mother in the town and shortly afterwards they moved to Belfast.

There was a succession of tenants but eventually the house lay empty until it was vested by the local council and demolished. Locals at that time believed that the presence had not entirely disappeared. At different times there have been sightings of a woman in white on the pathway along the River Foyle, which is popular with walkers and joggers. Some of these sightings have been known to be hoaxes but when one encounters the real ghost one is left in no doubt.

Redevelopment has changed the Foyle Road dramatically in the last years, and, although Mitchelburne Terrace is gone, some doubt that the ghost that dwelt in one of those houses would have ceased its haunting. In place of the old street is a new housing estate running from the end of the lower deck of Craigavon Bridge to the bottom of Southway, originally called the Old Coach Road. The Foyle Road has always had a reputation for being haunted and many still believe that it is.

In recent years nothing has been seen where the house once stood, so perhaps the spirit has found peace at last.

The Magherafelt Ghost

The road from Derry to Belfast has some of the most spectacular scenery anywhere in Ireland. At the breast of the Glenshane Pass a whole panorama opens up before you. On the right is the famed Slemish Mountain where St Patrick, as a young slave-boy, tended sheep. On the left are rolling hills but straight ahead, in the distance, one can see the sparkling waters of Lough Neagh, the largest freshwater lake in these islands. The road descends to the great plain of Ulster and the towns reflect this rich location: Maghera (from the Irish *Macaire Rátha* – plain of the ringfort) and Magherafelt (*Machaire Fíolta* – the plain of Fiolta).

It is hard to imagine that strange and hideous things could take place in such a lovely spot, but in the following case, poteen, the very potent illegally distilled whiskey, was at the heart of the cruel event. Poteen-making was common enough in most rural areas in Ireland around the time of the famine, and mid-Ulster was no different from anywhere else. It's said that once a man got the liking for the drink he would never give it up.

In the Magherafelt area, in the early part of the twentieth century, poteen was easy enough to find. One family, though, was particularly affected by it and this caused much distress to the wife. When her husband and two sons went on the drink they went berserk and became very violent, especially towards her. Neighbours predicted that it was bound to end in tragedy and it did.

One night, in the midst of a wild quarrel, the wife fell or was pushed down the stairs and died. Had it been one of the drunkards who had fallen down there would have been no eyebrows raised, but the wife was a sober God-fearing woman and unlikely to end her life like that. Neighbours believed that when she refused to give them money, her sons had pushed her and her body had been heard bouncing on every stair. The three swore that it was an accident and the police accepted it as such.

The father and the sons cleared off to England as soon as she was buried, leaving the house in the worst imaginable state. They made no attempt even to remove the blood from the stairs.

The neighbours were convinced that the house was haunted and no one would rent it, but the owners fixed it up and offered it at such a low rent that a lowly paid workman and his large family moved in. When they heard the rumours about it being haunted they dismissed them, saying that they weren't afraid, especially since it was a grand house for the rent.

For a while nothing untoward happened, until one night, around about the same time when the 'accident' had happened, the man and his wife were awakened by a very loud banging on the landing, followed by a thumping on the stairs which the man described as 'like a bag of coal being thrown from the top and thumping off each stair on the way down.' The same noises happened night after night without any let-up, and only the older members of the family seemed to hear them. The younger ones slept on undisturbed. After several nights of sleep deprivation, one of the older boys

and the father decided to sit at the bottom of the stairs to find out what exactly was going on. They lit candles, placed one on each stair and waited.

The silence was eerie, even sinister, the house was cold and the candles flickered. At midnight, one by one the candles were extinguished despite the air being still and calm without the hint of a draught. Then there was the loudest bang that, according to the father, 'made them jump nearly out of their skins'.

What happened next frightened them into leaving the house.

'We were sitting in the hall in total darkness and the thump-thump-thumping came down the stairs towards us. I tried to light a candle but as soon as it flared it went out, but not fast enough to hide what I saw! There was a woman with blood pouring out of her head and her face grotesquely twisted, lying at the foot of the stairs. I grabbed my son by the arm and pushed him into the living room. We were both petrified. We waited for what seemed an age and then I slowly opened the door. The hall was empty but that was it! We were moving out!'

They packed their things the next morning, and just before they left, the noises were ghastly and the house was filled with the most odious smell, yet it was curious that the only ones not affected were the two younger members of the family who casually gathered their bags and walked through the uproar.

Some time later that year, when the house was fixed up, new tenants moved in and there was a repeat of the happenings. They didn't stay long, saying that they had seen the ghost of a woman. Neighbours believed this to be the woman who was killed.

The house was later demolished.

The Caring Spirit of Nassau Street

Nassau Street is in Rosemount, the area of the city that used to be known as 'The Village'. The people were said to be clannish – this was not an insult, rather it was an indication that they looked out for each other, took care of each other when needed and were supportive in times of trouble. I believe that this is at the heart of a story that I heard concerning a mother and her sick child.

The couple lived in Nassau Street in one of the small terraced houses and considered themselves fortunate to have a place to themselves. The husband was a soldier in the Irish Army and was away from home quite often. Although his wife missed him, she had a new baby and this took up much of her time.

In late October the baby developed a cough and a high temperature.

In a small terrace house in Nassau Street, in the Rosemount area, a ghostly nurse watched.

The medicine prescribed by the doctor didn't seem to help and the baby cried constantly right into the early hours of the morning. Not wanting to call the doctor out, the mother hoped that if she gave the baby a bottle of milk he would settle. She went downstairs to the little scullery and while she was waiting for the water to boil she heard some movement above her.

Now the small room above the kitchen was empty except for boxes and general stuff still to be unpacked since they moved in, yet she distinctly heard the creaking of floorboards. She listened and the sound was as if someone was walking across the room above, over and back, over and back, with a very steady tread. She went to the bottom of the stairs to listen but all was quiet except for the soft whimpering of the baby. She thought that perhaps she might be mistaken and that the sound was coming from the house next door.

She made up the bottle, one of those glass boat-shaped ones with a teat on both ends, with National Dried Milk formula and left the scullery. When she entered the living room and walked towards the open door to the stairs, she stopped and stared. A woman was standing on the last stair but what shocked the mother was the fact that she seemed to be almost transparent. The mother was able to see the Sacred Heart picture with its glowing red lamp on the wall behind the woman. Terrified, she dropped the baby's bottle, which smashed on the tiled floor. She jumped back and looked down and when she raised her eyes again the woman was gone.

She ran to the hall but there was no sign of the woman. She checked the front door: it was still securely bolted. When she realised that there was no crying from the bedroom she took the stairs two at a time to check on her baby, and all sorts of scary thoughts were running through her mind. At the bedroom door she stopped, blessed herself and said a silent prayer that her baby wasn't dead. She tiptoed to the cot and the child was sleeping peacefully. She felt his forehead and the fever seemed to have gone. She bent her head to listen to the baby's breathing and it was unlaboured and steady.

She sank to her knees and said a prayer in thanksgiving. She had no doubt that the woman's form that had passed her had something to do with her baby's recovery.

The next morning when she lifted the baby into her arms a tiny soft toy that she knew she hadn't yet unpacked was lying in the cot. Later that day, when she went into the small room, the boxes were still stacked neatly on the floor except for the one that had held the baby's things.

She phoned her husband from a neighbour's house and when she finished the call her neighbour said, 'I couldn't help hearing what you were saying. You know a nurse used to live in that house and she lost her baby to meningitis. Maybe she was just looking out for you.'

The mother never saw the woman again and her son is now a strapping big man.

The Priest's House

If you walk along Bishop Street, through Bishop Gate in the Derry Walls, and continue just past Abercorn Road you will come to Ferguson's Lane. It is a small, some would say insignificant street but in the 1770s Father John Lynch, who was to make a lasting impression on the city, lived there, and it was said that when he died his ghost continued to reside in that place.

He was a native of Balteagh, Dungiven, a theological graduate of the Sorbonne in Paris and, eventually, the parish priest of Derry at that time. In 1783, thanks to the inspiration of Father Lynch, the present Long Tower Church began life, though on a much smaller scale than it is at present. Unfortunately he did not live to see his church completed for he died very suddenly during Christmas week in 1785, just a few short weeks before the opening ceremonies took place. In Ferguson's Lane, he often celebrated Mass in his house and, when weather permitted, near the Hawthorn tree, which marked the traditional site of the Teampall Mór, the great Cathedral of Derry. His death saddened the whole Catholic community because Father John was a man who believed in ecumenism, and in his fundraising campaign for the building of the church he received £200 from Dr Hervey, Earl of Bristol and the then-Protestant Bishop of Derry. From the Londonderry Corporation he received £50.

His own house was neither ornate nor extravagant but it served its purpose as a centre for young priests or students for the priesthood to gather for Mass, discussion and tuition. In the largest room there was a semi-circular cupboard, which was specifically to store vestments and the items needed for the celebration of Mass.

The house was divided into two dwellings when the Sisters of Nazareth inherited it, and the small square was renamed McLaughlin's Close after the constructor who built more houses on the site. The original features of the seminary, the small curving staircase, the cornices and the upstairs fireplaces were still evident when the final tenants left.

The families who lived there had several ghostly experiences over the years but they maintained that they were mostly benign manifestations. Still, as one resident said, 'Any ghostly happening is frightening when you're not expecting it.'

One of the young daughters was asleep in bed when something woke her up. She felt the mattress depress as if someone had sat on the side of the bed, but when she tried to open her eyes to see who it might be she couldn't.

She said, 'I felt as if I was paralysed, I know I tried to ask who it was but even my voice wasn't working. I tried to raise my hand to my face but it remained by my side. It was the most terrifying feeling because I just knew that there was someone sitting on my bed, even though I couldn't hear any breathing.'

When the weight arose off the bed she found that she was able to move and call out for her brother who was downstairs.

All that remains of the Priest's House is an empty yard bordered on one side by the retaining walls. Beneath the flagstones lay a secret passage.

He came rushing out of the sitting room into the hall, followed by their little terrier, but when he reached the bottom of the stairs the dog started to bark wildly and then backed into the corner whimpering and cowering. The brother stepped on the bottom stair but he could move no further.

'I fell backwards,' he said, 'as if someone pushed me, but there was no one there. All I remember is that it was freezing cold!' When his sister screamed again he attempted to go upstairs once more and this time he succeeded. He found her in hysterics and babbling about a ghost.

The terrier refused ever after that to go upstairs even though he had always slept in the girl's room until then.

Some years later another son opened the front door and walked in only to be confronted by a figure dressed in a long black robe and a wide-brimmed hat. His face was indistinct and he moved, almost floating, through the hall wall at the place where a door once was before the house was divided into two. The figure neither looked nor seemed conscious of anyone watching. The boy, however, stood rooted to the spot and slowly breathed out. He wondered if he had just been seeing things, but later his mother assured him that 'your man was a frequent visitor when I prayed for a wee bit of help.' After that he felt no fear when he saw the spirit.

In the adjacent house the woman wanted a clothes line put up in her yard. Her husband used a crowbar and sledgehammer to break a hole through the concrete. On the third punch with the hammer the crowbar suddenly disappeared through the new hole and by the sound it made it was clear that it had fallen into a deep empty space. When an engineer came to inspect what had happened, he said that he suspected it was an underground passage, possibly leading to the church. Unfortunately that could not be confirmed and the opening was cemented over, but this event did perhaps explain to the occupants why they had, on occasion, seen an eerie figure at that very spot. It might have been a passage that Fr Lynch used to go to see the Long Tower Church building taking shape.

The house was demolished in the 1970s, despite many people objecting to the destruction of such an old and historic building.

The site today is fenced off, a forlorn tiled square with dogs safely guarding it.

Let us hope that the spirits that dwelt there found their rest.

The Soldier's Ghost

There are some strange stories about ghosts in the army but none as strange as the one that followed a soldier from India back to Derry. The story began in the first quarter of the twentieth century far away from Ireland, somewhere near the north-west frontier of India.

Irish soldiers serving in the British Army in India at that time faced many conflicts of loyalty. The Easter Rising had already taken place in 1916. Sixteen of the leaders were executed and the Irish War of Independence followed from 1919 to 1921. Many of the 250,000 men that Ireland provided for the First World War were serving in India.

When news reached them of the brutalities of the 'Black and Tans' towards their fellow countrymen and women, 400 men revolted and refused to carry out orders issued by their officers. This was a courageous but foolhardy stand against the authority of the army and earned them the name of 'The Devil's Own'.

When the terms of surrender of the mutineers were eventually reached, they were taken to a camp far from the army post and had to live in tents, under the cruel heat of the Indian sun. This, however, was the least of their problems. Daily their lives were threatened by the patrolling guards who, urged on by their officers, beat and starved the prisoners and condemned them to live in conditions that were often worse than those of animals that roamed the countryside.

Some of the soldiers attempted to escape and it is believed that during one such attempt one of the cruellest officers was killed. It was never discovered what actually happened and the Irishmen were a loyal bunch, particularly in this case. The army suspected foul play but could not prove it, so later it retaliated in another part of India, Dagshai, and executed fourteen men by firing squad for their part in the mutiny.

The death of this most despicable officer and his ghostly reappearance is at the heart of the story played out in the Waterside area of Derry. When the soldiers returned home to Ireland, one of them came to stay with his sister in Derry. Very soon neighbours living in the same row of houses began to hear strange sounds at all hours of the day and night. They noticed that the lights in the house were never switched off. The ex-soldier took to walking the streets, speaking angrily, as if to some invisible companion. He began to get the name of being 'not being quite right in the head'.

Most startling of all was the change that came over his sister. While he was in the army she worked in one of the shirt factories and was known to be a very sociable person, but when her brother returned she inexplicably withdrew from the company of her friends. Of course they speculated about the change, and when her dark wavy hair began to turn to grey and then white within a few short months they were even more concerned.

When she didn't turn up at work for a few days, one of her close friends decided to visit her to check if she was ill. When she knocked on the door no one answered although she heard movements within the house. She went to the window but the curtains were closed. Still worried, she bent down and looked through the letterbox. There was no one in the hallway but right up the stairs on both walls there were red lamps and what appeared to be pictures of the Sacred Heart. She called and hammered on the door again and eventually her friend opened it. Later, when describing the scene to her fellow workers, Kate broke down and cried.

'Margaret opened the door about 6 inches and I almost didn't recognise her. Her white hair looked as if she'd never run a comb through it. Her eyes were sunk in her head, you'd think she hadn't slept for a month and that brother of hers was standing right behind her. I don't like the look of it at all. We've got to find out what's going on.'

The following week, true to her word, she persuaded her brother Charlie, who knew the ex-soldier from schooldays, to invite him to their house in Alfred Street. Much to their surprise, he came. Charlie gave him a hearty welcome and Kate went to the kitchen to make a cup of tea. Within minutes a loud knocking came to their front door.

Kate went out but there was no one there. A few minutes later the knock came again, louder this time. Again she opened the front door and no one was there. She looked up and down the street but it was empty. She turned to close the door but she felt a blast of hot, fetid air around her and she was pushed back against the wall with some force.

'I was that frightened,' she said later, 'that I couldn't move and when I heard that poor soldier howling it fairly terrified me. Charlie called me and I went into our parlour and he was trying to hold his friend down on the chair but he just kept saying, "I have to leave, I have to leave."'

'Why, for God's sake? Sure you just got here?'

'It's him. He won't leave me alone. He's always there.' He pointed to the corner of the room but it was empty.

'Who is?' I asked, for as sure as I'm standing here, he scared me.

'That officer.' He pointed to the corner. 'He's tormenting me!'

Charlie told me to go and get the sister and I ran up the street but she was already on her way down.

'He followed him there, didn't he? I didn't want him to go but he thought maybe he'd get peace for a while.'

'Who or what are you talking about? There was no one else in the house but your brother and he went a bit berserk shouting and pointing.'

She ran right into our house. She took a wee bottle of holy water from her pocket and started to sprinkle it around our parlour, saying prayers all the while. Her brother calmed down after a while and then he stood up.

'I have to go,' he said, calmly this time, and Margaret helped him on with his coat. She ushered him out of the house but before she left she whispered, 'I'll explain later. Thanks anyway for inviting him.'

A few days later she came to the door of the house in Alfred Street. Her story was a strange one. Apparently her brother was one of the soldiers caught up in the mutiny. The officer drew his pistol to shoot them, but being unarmed and fearing for their lives her brother and three others jumped on him and overpowered him. When he didn't get up they thought that they just knocked him out but blood began to stain the dry soil of the camp and they realised that he was dead. They managed to hide him in the bushes behind the camp. When his body was found the next day, ravaged by wild animals, they hoped it would be accepted as an accident. But the ghost of the dead officer haunted her brother from that time onwards.

In the beginning no one believed her, thinking that she and her brother were mentally disturbed, but a priest was persuaded to come to the house to bless it and he was shocked to be able to see the ghost of the officer, dressed in his walking-out uniform. His blank eyes stared at the priest and then he smiled a horrible evil grin. The priest, despite being faced with the malevolent manifestation, walked to the stairs, blessing the house as he went. The spectral figure appeared ahead of him and stood as if to block his way. The priest continued his exorcism but the spirit refused to leave the house. The priest told the sister to place blessed candles in each room and on the stairs and to use holy water each time the spirit appeared.

Margaret never returned to work. She stayed at home to care for her brother. The hauntings continued until her brother died. The same priest was there at his bedside and gave him the last rites of the Church. He was buried without fuss in the city cemetery. Later she heard that the ghost also haunted the other participants in the death.

5

HAUNTED BUILDINGS

THERE are haunted buildings in every town and city. Although we try to discover the reason for the haunting, it often escapes us. Perhaps there is no logical reason, but sometimes, just sometimes, the reason is secreted within their history.

The First Derry National School (The Verbal Arts Centre)

During the time when the First Derry National School functioned as a centre for education, it had its own ghost. The school was built just within the City Walls beside Bishop Gate and is now one of the many listed buildings within the old city.

It catered for the young children of the city and also offered a welcome and education to the cabin boys of ships berthed in Derry. Although the teachers and headmasters were generally very well thought of, it is suspected that in its early years one of teachers was a very strict disciplinarian and not as kindly as the rest of the staff. His discipline was harsh as it was in many institutions at that time, and he was known to act out his dislike on some of the pupils.

Looking into the history of the building, we can only speculate that one of the boys suffered some brutal punishment and that it is he who now haunts the top floor.

The school was generally considered excellent and was famous for its Blue Coat Choir: when the boys sang in the Church services, dressed in their blue coats and yellow britches, their voices were so exquisite that people came from all over the town to hear them.

One of the most famous people to attend the first school built on that site was playwright George Farquhar (c. 1677–1707), who turned to writing after he accidently wounded a fellow actor in a staged sword fight. The Ulster History Circle recognised his popularity as a playwright by erecting a blue plaque on the site. *Love and a Bottle*, his first comedy, was produced at Drury Lane in 1698 and enjoyed a fair degree of popularity, but his most famous plays were *The Recruiting Officer* and *The Beaux' Stratagem*.

In 1894, when the old building became no longer fit for purpose, a new school – the present one – was built, but obviously the ghost still hovered around because there were reports that passers-by had strange experiences as they entered and left the old city by Bishop Gate. Some were inclined to say that it was the soldiers who were managing the checkpoint at that time playing tricks, but it would be quite difficult to simulate floating black forms and produce icy rushes of air in the middle of summer.

In the year 2000, the refurbishment of the school was completed and the Verbal Arts Centre, dedicated to the promotion of the written and spoken word, moved there. It would appear that the resident ghost did not leave during the renovation, and it made its presence felt to a staff member who was working late in the building rearranging the blue room after a meeting. It was very late and all of the other workers had gone home. However, he was quite content going about his work until something strange began to happen. He felt the room growing very, very cold and shivered, logically thinking that the heating had been turned off early or that a window was open. He examined each window but they were closed tightly, so still not too perturbed he turned to get his sweater, which he'd left downstairs, before he went home.

He said, 'I stopped short because at that second I felt as if an icicle was dangling over me, ready to fall. My breath formed a vapour in the air, which felt stifling even though it was freezing cold. It was just not a normal feeling and I could hardly catch my breath. I swear I thought I was going to pass out! I left the room, got my sweater and made myself a good strong cup of coffee downstairs. When I felt warm again I decided to tackle the blue room again and went back upstairs,' he continued. 'I was rearranging chairs when I caught sight of something out of the corner of my eye. When you see something moving you naturally turn to see what it is. Well, I wish I hadn't because what I saw scared the living daylights out of me.'

He said that something, some form like a smallish black cloak, floated very silently across the room and disappeared through the wall towards the larger room on the right while he watched in a state of horror and confusion. 'It was as if a presence was somehow swirling all the air out of the room. I was so scared,' he said, 'that I started to bang the chairs onto the table and make as much noise as I could.'

He decided to get out of the building as soon as he could, but when he went downstairs and began to turn off the lights before leaving, the lift doors suddenly opened. They stayed like that for a moment or two and then closed. 'The coldness that I had felt upstairs seemed to follow me downstairs in the foyer. I was so petrified that I was almost paralysed. I was breathing deeply and my

Many pupils and teachers passed through the old First Derry School National School. Do their ghost still haunt the Verbal Arts Centre?

heart was beating nineteen to the dozen. I can tell you that I have never been so frightened in all my life.'

The next day he began to think that perhaps he had overreacted to being alone in the building, but one of the other employees related much the same experience of the lift doors opening and closing and of hearing a weird whispering in the corner of that room. The first worker had not mentioned the whispering and was shocked to hear that her experience was exactly like his the previous night.

Could there be other institutions in the town where the spirits of victims of brutal punishments continue to haunt?

Until the 1970s, corporal punishment was the main form of discipline in schools and many of them would have had a reputation for harsh discipline. It is to be hoped that the joyful sounds of children who attend the various functions now in the Verbal Arts Centre will neutralise any sad memories of those who have gone before.

The Ghost of the Bakery

There was a Georgian house situated where the Cultúrlann is now, in Great James Street. From the outside it looked just like any other house – tall and narrow with three windows on each floor. But if you had looked at it closely you would have seen that it did not have a pitched roof like the other houses. It was flat.

'Why is that?' one might ask. And therein lies the ghostly tale.

At the end of the nineteenth century, an old woman and her servant lived there. As they both grew older they were unable to look after the house. The carpets were worn and the colour faded from the curtains in the light. The old furniture was seldom dusted but in the candle light at night things like that did not matter.

Then, one cold autumn evening, as night crept in, the servant lit the fire to heat the room for her mistress. A cinder sparked out onto the carpet and set it alight. She screamed and tried to extinguish the blaze but didn't succeed. Terrified, she ran to the drawing room and called for her mistress. But because of age and ill health, the mistress could not come down.

The servant did her best to save her mistress, but unfortunately before long the whole house was in flames and the two women were trapped inside. The neighbours were horrified when they saw the leaping flames illuminating the darkness of the night sky.

One night, seven years to the day when the house went on fire, a carriage was passing by that place. The horse reared up on its hind legs, foaming at the mouth. When the coachman looked up he saw two figures at the top window of the shell of the house. Screams filled the air and the frightened horse galloped off.

Over the years, people reported seeing the ghosts and hearing cries and screams, particularly in the loneliness of the night. There were many stories; people spoke of strange noises, rustling and whispering, coming from the burnt house. In the end, the house fell into disrepair and in 1936 it was restored and converted into a bakery.

Years passed and there were no reports of the ghosts until one night, before Halloween, something very strange happened. The workers in the bakery were working night and day baking apple pies, barmbracks and other seasonal fare for Halloween.

Around four o'clock in the morning during their tea break, a burning smell permeated the large room. At the same time the air became icy cold, and when they looked up they saw an old woman and another shadowy figure. The old woman beckoned to the workers to follow them. Only one man moved forward; the others stood in petrified silence. He followed the women into the main room at the back of the bakery, which housed the huge ovens.

It was obvious that one had overheated and was in danger of going on fire. The man hurried to disconnect the oven and when the danger was passed turned to thank the women but they had disappeared. The Cultúrlann now stands on that site and no strange apparitions were ever seen from that day to this.

The notorious thirteen steps to the old Waterside Workhouse where ghosts wandered at will.

The Ghost-Ridden Waterside Workhouse

The old workhouse on Glendermott Road in the Waterside was an eerie-looking place and must have struck fear into those who dragged themselves up the thirteen steps to its forbidding entrance.

It was built in 1840 to accommodate about 800 inmates, but when the dreadful famine swept through Ireland in the mid-1840s the number swelled to 1,200. For most, the workhouse was the last resort, preferable only to death, but for many inmates who lived there death was a welcome release from the hard grind and inhumane conditions.

Men, women and children were segregated and housed in different parts of the building. All suffered under a harsh, authoritarian regime. This is the basis for the story of 'The Blue Matron of the Waterside Workhouse' and it does not lose its horror in the re-telling.

The guardian at the centre of the story, known as the 'matron in blue', was responsible for the welfare of the children. She showed little mercy and was quite rigid in her application of the workhouse rules. If a child infringed any of these rules she meted out the punishment. Perhaps she too was a victim of circumstance because it is said that in the early days of her appointment, the Board of Management of the workhouse brought her to book for being too lenient, and after that her adherence to ruling 'by the book' became a byword.

From that time on she applied punishment severely and without partiality. One of her punishments was to lock a recalcitrant child in a large cupboard under the stairs until he or she 'learnt their lesson'. It was isolated enough for any screams or crying not to be heard.

One cold winter's night, two poor sisters cried piteously for their mother. They were inconsolable and eventually the matron heard of it. She sent one of the staff to bring them to her and the girl did so reluctantly. The matron began a tirade, which only made the children cry harder. When she screamed at them that they were going to be sent to 'the hole', their cries could be heard throughout that wing of the building. The matron hustled them roughly towards the stairs, and although they promised to be good she pushed them into the cupboard with neither light nor heat.

A short time later, the matron received word that her sister in County Derry was seriously ill. She packed quickly and left, forgetting about the children. The weather turned colder and she decided to stay until her sister was on the mend. It was only when she was preparing to return to the workhouse that she remembered about the children.

More afraid for her reputation than for the two little sisters, she frantically urged the coachman to return as quickly as possible to the workhouse, all the while dreading what she would find when she arrived. Her worst fears were confirmed when she dashed to the stairs. Not a sound was to be heard from the cupboard. She hoped and prayed that someone had released them, but when she opened the door she found the two children clinging to each other, both of them dead from cold, thirst and hunger. The piteous spectacle shocked her to the core and the enormity of what she had done hit her.

She was heartsick and she wept bitter, bitter tears, realising how pitiless she had become. No one could console her and the knowledge preyed on her until she lost her mind. It is said that she became

a demented shadow of herself and she walked the corridors of the workhouse, searching every room, opening and closing doors and weeping, trying to find the now long-dead children. Full of remorse she finally gave up the will to live.

But her spirit could not rest in peace. Soon her ghost was seen walking the corridors of the workhouse, opening doors and lamenting the great wrong that she'd done. The inmates fled when they saw this deranged spectre, and this awful visit from the grave was harder to bear than all the indignities they suffered living in the unspeakable conditions of the workhouse.

It is said that an attempt to exorcise the matron's spirit ended in failure, for when the priest tried to remove it from the building it became pandemoniac, forcing the exorcist from side to side until he was exhausted. Finally he was able to commit the spirit to the old dispensary and the door was locked.

When the building became a hospital, the night nurses often had fleeting glimpses of her. Nurse Canning told me that when she was a young nurse working in the hospital, she took ill and underwent an operation. She woke up very cold in the early hours of the morning and was aware of a woman, dressed in blue, placing an extra blanket on the bed. The woman's features were not distinct but the patient recalled that her hands were gentle. She tucked the blanket in around the bed before disappearing through the wall of the room.

She also told me about a more recent matron called Edwards. She had a small flat within the grounds where one night, without warning, doors began to open and close and water started pouring out of all the taps. She tried to turn them off but each one refused to turn. The water gushed out with even greater ferocity, frightening her so much that she ran from the hospital and never lived there again.

The workhouse was turned into a wonderful museum and library, yet few people dare to stay alone too long in its corridors. The bones of the many bodies that were found in the paupers' grave in the workhouse grounds in the 1990s were given a Christian burial in Ballyoan Cemetery. Yet there is still an air of sadness about the place and we are left wondering if the guardian and the children of her unintentional crime have now reached a place of peaceful rest together.

The Limavady Workhouse where nurses still tend their non-existent patients. (Courtesy of LCDI Limavady)

Limavady Workhouse Spirits

Limavady Workhouse opened in 1842, just before the worst famine in Irish history. It is a severe-looking building like most workhouses, and people had to be in the deepest despair before they would enter its doors. When they got accepted, and not all did, they were worked to the bone. It is reported that at least ten people died each week, most from overwork and starvation. Since men and their wives and children were separated on entering according to gender, there have been tales of the spirits of women weeping for their husbands and children.

One sighting of a ghost happened just a few years ago when a film crew was surveying the building for a documentary in the area that was originally the women's dormitory, which was in the top-left wing of the workhouse. At least 200 women would have been crowded into this room and would have slept on straw on top of bare floorboards.

The film crew had been working for about an hour with a spirit medium whom they had asked to make contact with the spirit world, when a presence responded to the call. The spirit banged on the floor twice and when asked to repeat the contact it again thumped the floor twice. The crew captured the sound, and even though this was the purpose of the documentary they confessed to being frightened by the response.

In 1932 the workhouse was converted to the district hospital, and some of the unexplained sightings would seem to date from that time. Also, according to Damian Corr, the manager of the building, which is now the home of the Limavady Community Development Initiative (LCDI). He told the following story:

'There was a table in the foyer where our security guards used to sit and at the end of the left-hand corridor where the maternity ward used to be they regularly reported hearing the sound of babies crying. These sounds were quite distressing to listen to but when the guards approached the crying ceased.'

Damian has many other tales to tell and a lot of them are about the spirits of nurses who possibly worked there. The most harrowing one is of a young nurse who was pregnant and unmarried. She was able to hide the pregnancy, but when the time came to deliver her baby she killed it, so afraid was she of the shame. Later, wracked with remorse for the terrible deed she had done, she hanged herself, and her spirit wanders the corridors, bewailing the death of her baby.

Local folklore has the tale that a person believed to be a nurse walks the corridor of the nurses' home every morning at three o'clock. The tapping sound one hears resembles the walk of someone with a wooden leg, rather a strange disability for a nurse to have. One patient heard the footfalls coming into the ward, right to her bed, where they stopped, but when she looked up there was no one there. This happened quite often to other patients as well.

In the 1960s and 1970s there were several sightings of a nurse in the old-fashioned uniform and cape with a red hood sitting on the bridge at the front of the hospital.

The daytime security guard Evan Hand was alone in the building recently when he had a terrifying encounter. He saw a shadow in the reception area, and thinking it was a car drawing up outside he looked out; however, there was no car. A movement caught his eyes and when he turned to look he saw a shadow moving up the stairs. When he followed the shadow it vanished at the turn of the stairwell, but there was a pervading sense of unease left.

'I was really scared,' he said. 'It was something not normal.'

A photograph was taken by one of the security guards at the LCDI, and has been authenticated by Paranormal Society Ireland. On close inspection it would seem to be a woman and child. The woman was wearing bonnet-style clothing, an attire closely linked to the period the building hails from.

The Old Convent

Gathering ghost stories and taking photographs of haunted places can be a weird and terrifying thing to do. I have been to some strange and eerie places but one in particular stands out in my mind.

It had been whispered that the old deserted convent building in the centre of town was haunted, but I needed to take a suitably eerie photograph inside it to illustrate the article I was writing.

It was a cold blustery afternoon in late autumn and dead leaves crawled like crabs along the pavement. Moss-covered steps led to the peeling door and it took both my hands to turn the huge rusted key. I stepped inside the high-ceilinged hall and the slamming of the warped oak door behind me echoed loudly in the silence. I switched on the light and a single bulb without a shade dangled on a thin cable from the ceiling. Its light barely lit up the gloom.

I switched on my flashlight and looked around. Dried-out spiders clung to the cobwebs and as I stepped onto the bottom stair something landed on my head and tangled in my hair. Even as a child I had a huge distaste of spiders, and in spite of my bravery at entering there alone I found myself whimpering and frantically trying to sweep off, shuddering at the thought of what it might be. In my panic I dropped my torchlight and it shut off. I fumbled for the switch but nothing happened.

My inner voice was saying, 'Get out of here,' but I couldn't leave. I had to take a photograph. Earlier I had reassured myself that I could do this: after all, I'd been here before, although not alone. I promised myself that I would be quick as I began to climb the wide staircase. It was a spooky experience and the sound echoed upwards with the creak of every stair. I felt a draught of cold air as I reached the five stairs that the ghost of a nun was reported to haunt. Heart thudding, I bolted up the next flights that were narrow and seemed to be in various stages of decay.

The only light in the top corridor shone through the old doors of the nuns' cells. I moved to the end of the passageway to a larger room that was bare, with peeling walls, but it had what I wanted – three windows with shutters, looking out onto Pump Street. This would be the ideal image for the story of the haunted convent. I set my camera to a slow-shutter speed and braced myself against a wall to avoid a shake. I wanted a perfect photograph and as I moved backwards to

Pump Street where ghosts wander, especially in the Old Convent.

get the right angle I sensed something behind me.

'One minute and I'll be done,' I told myself, but before I could press the shutter I felt a gentle push on my back. Forgetting that I was alone I shouted angrily, 'Stop pushing me!'

There was no answer and it dawned on me that someone or something else was in the room. I gasped and swung around, but the room was empty.

Beneath me the floor creaked, and when I looked down I saw that the floorboards were split and in a very dangerous condition. The reality of it hit me. If I had not been pushed I would probably have fallen and hurt myself badly, and no one would have known where I was. The Lord alone knows how long I might have had to wait for someone to come. I shivered at the thought.

I didn't wait to take the photograph. I took the stairs three at a time and stumbled into the darkening street, my camera swinging from my shoulder. I ran to my car, disappointed to miss getting a photograph but greatly relieved to be out of the building. I returned the key the next day.

'Did you get a good photograph?' I was asked.

I shook my head. 'Bad light,' I muttered.

'Ah well, sure you can try again,' he said.

'No way,' I thought. Still, I was so disappointed that I would not have an image for the haunted convent story.

Next day as I transferred the photographs to my computer something again gave me the shivers. There it was – filling the screen – a striking photograph of the three windows: a photograph I believe I hadn't taken.

The room where the benign ghost resides.

The Haunting of the Hall

Before St Columb's Hall was built in 1888 as a Temperance Hall, McFeeley's Livery Stables were ensconced there. Even earlier, the Pear Tree Inn was an establishment of some importance because of its situation so close to the Derry Walls and Reid's Market.

Traditionally, the priests of the Long Tower church managed it until it was sold recently. The last manager told of a ghostly experience and one that he would rather forget. One night he received a telephone call from a woman reporting that she had heard the sound of breaking glass as she passed by St Columb's Hall. It was about 11.30 p.m. by the time the priest and the caretaker arrived to check out if all was well. They decided not to contact the police, thinking that the woman may have been mistaken or that it was just a bit of carry-on by some young boys passing by. Before they went inside they checked that there were no broken windows or other damage on the outside. When they were satisfied, they entered the building by the main front door, locking it behind them.

The priest knew every room and corner of the building and when he made his usual nightly checks he switched off each light as he left. Unerringly he was able to go from one room to another checking that each door was locked before leaving the premises.

When he came to the last light in the foyer he used a flashlight for the final locking up.

'Why don't we just separate and check? It'll be quicker,' suggested the caretaker.

Separating from each other, they made a tour of the building but all windows were securely fastened, intact and undisturbed. They unlocked the internal doors and relocked them again as they checked each room.

When they met up again in the main foyer they decided that the woman must have been mistaken and they turned to leave. At that moment there was an almighty bang that almost made the building shudder.

'I felt the floor tremble,' said the priest, 'and at first I thought it was an explosion in the town, but the noise seemed to come from inside the building and was too close for it to be outside.'

The priest knew that only the heavy door to the ballroom could possibly have made that particular sound (though,

to his knowledge, never loud enough or hard enough to shake the building). He rushed downstairs followed by the caretaker. When they arrived at the solid wooden double door to the ballroom the priest tried the handle. It was firmly locked!

He wanted to be certain that it was the slamming of this door that had made the terrible bang they'd heard, so he unlocked it, put the key in his pocket and suggested to the caretaker that one of them should return to the foyer and the other would slam the door to make sure that this was the cause of the bang. He asked the caretaker, who was by now as nervous as he was, to slam the door when he was sure that the priest had reached the foyer. He took the stairs two at a time.

St Columb's Hall, a much-loved venue for entertainment in the 1960s and '70s but earlier ghosts claim it when the audience departs.

A few moments later, he shouted that he was in the foyer. The caretaker slammed the door as hard as he could. The sound reverberated through the building but was certainly not as severe or loud as before. The priest returned downstairs to relock the door, aware that his companion did not like being there on his own. As he passed the turn of the stairs he saw some dark form take shape and begin to move deep in the shadows. He felt a cold, clammy, invisible presence beginning to creep eerily around him and the hairs rose on the back of his neck. He described the sensation as a disembodied mass that seemed to detach itself from the walls and stairs. When he passed it he felt the iciness creep right into his bones.

When he reached the caretaker he was so nervous that he couldn't say anything, so strong was the feeling. Holding the key tightly in both hands, he relocked the door. It was the only key to that lock; there were no duplicates, which made the slamming of that door even more eerie.

He couldn't explain to himself how a locked door could open itself, slam shut with such deadly ferocity and relock itself. Just in case he was imagining things he asked the caretaker to check that the door was indeed locked before they left to go upstairs. He noticed that when his companion passed the shadowy corner he shivered and hastened on.

'Let's get out of here,' he said, 'this place gives me the creeps at night.' They made a quick exit through the front door and returned to their respective houses.

The next morning, wanting to reassure himself that nothing else untoward had happened during the night, the priest asked one of the staff to accompany him to examine the door in daylight. He turned the handle, expecting it still to be locked, but the handle turned easily. The door was once again mysteriously unlocked.

Later he heard that others felt quite uncomfortable and uneasy as they sensed the same eerie presence at the stairwell, particularly during the dark winter evenings when natural light did not reach into the shadows.

St Columb's Hall lay unused for some time until it was temporarily taken over by the Playhouse during their renovations. That staff too sensed something strange and foreboding in the downstairs area of the Hall.

Was this spooky experience a reaction or resistance to the disuse of the Hall as a place of entertainment? Was it an imaginary occurrence enhanced by the lateness of the hour and the emptiness of the building? Those who felt it could say not.

One must also look to the early history of the site. Who knows what might have happened to a traveller staying in the Pear Tree Inn, for we know that unexpected things happened to the unwary.

The Opera House Phantom

As a student I developed a great interest in drama and theatre, and when I returned to Derry I was delighted and intrigued to meet an old man who had worked in the Opera House on Carlisle Road in Derry.

Thomas was a young man in 1911. He was a well-qualified mechanic and much in demand for cars, which were quite a novelty then, but he was persuaded to earn some extra money by taking care of the general maintenance, theatre lighting and sound effects in the building. No one told him that there was a ghost in residence.

Once the pride of the city, the Opera House mysteriously burned down on 9 March 1940. (Bigger/MacDonald Collection, courtesy of NI Libraries)

'If I'd known that,' he said, 'I would have run a mile, but I'm glad I didn't because that ghost was a real gentleman!'

He described the Opera House as a magnificent first-class theatre of which any city could be proud. It was the realisation of a dream for James F. Warden from Hull to bring such a facility to Derry. It opened on 10 August 1877 with a gala evening and an excited audience. It was built on a well-considered site with the rear entrance on John Street, which was at a lower level than the frontage onto Carlisle Road. This meant that everything needed for the shows that came to Derry could be loaded and unloaded through this goods entrance, a very innovative idea in the late nineteenth century. The stage

sets could be hoisted to the stage level of the theatre and at the end of a run they could be quickly transported for the next booking. Overseeing this was one of the many duties that Barney Armstrong, the manager of the Opera House, entrusted to Thomas.

When Thomas was in his late 70s he recounted a story about a ghostly encounter containing such a wealth of detail that it seemed as fresh in his mind as if it had happened just the day before.

Before a performance I had to set up the lights, make sure that the backdrops and scenery for each act could be moved easily and that props were in place. One morning early I was having a tricky time trying to untangle the rope of the mechanical hoist. It hadn't been working properly the previous day and there was a new setting ready to be put into place. Well, I thought I was on my own and was muttering that I could do with a bit of help when I felt a tap on my shoulder. I couldn't turn around because I was in an awkward position so I just said, 'Can you give me a hand with this?' Within a few moments with the extra pair of hands helping, the hoist was fixed and I turned to thank whoever it was for his help but the stage was completely empty. There was no one there. I couldn't understand it because there wasn't time for anyone to disappear.

He called out but no one answered. He went onto the stage and called again but his voice echoed back from the silent auditorium. He kept calling and searched around, front and backstage but there was no sign of another person there.

He checked the three large doors in the front and the doors at the back but they were securely locked. He methodically searched the dressing rooms, which occupied two floors, the box office and manager's office in the vestibule. When he climbed the ornate staircase to the balcony and dress circle he heard some sounds behind him as if someone was following him, but again when he turned around he could see no one. Finally he climbed the stone steps to the 'gods' and looked down to the theatre floor far below. There was no sign of anyone. When he called again he swore that he heard a chuckle from behind. By this time he was getting both annoyed and a little nervous so he hurriedly descended to the stage level to finish off his setting-up as quickly as possible before he left.

Thomas was the sort of person who looked for a practical explanation to everything, but on this occasion there was none. That evening, after the performance, he mentioned his experience to Mr Armstrong, who just shrugged his shoulders and said, 'You're not the only one who has spoken of the ghost. When Miss King (one of the leading ladies in a show that came to town) was in her dressing room putting on her make-up at the mirror, she saw the reflection of a man sitting on the chair in the corner. She was really annoyed and turned around to demand why he was in her dressing room but there was no one there. Strange to say she gave a great performance that night but she gave me a terrible time about the ghost.'

Thomas nodded and said that he wasn't frightened but just grateful for the help. That was the one and only time that he experienced anything like that. He finished the story by saying, 'There were many occasions when I needed help after that but "your man" ignored me!'

6

HAUNTED PLACES

OFTEN we walk along a road or enter a strange situation and something feels out of place. We can't say exactly what it is but there is something gnawing at the edge of our consciousness that creates an uneasy feeling. We need to ask ourselves if we are treading on ghostly ground.

The Old Coach Road and John 'Terror' Scott

In the nineteenth century, a gentleman, by social standing only, was nicknamed John 'Terror' Scott because of his cruel and vicious temper. When he was young, his father, Captain William Scott, a retired army officer, an autocrat and the owner of Foyle Hill House and lands, gave in to his son's every whim and John grew up believing that he could do whatever he wished without suffering any consequences. As a young man yet to reach his majority, John careered around the countryside on a black horse that was as temperamental as its owner. When he went into town he generally took the coach and drove the horses down the Coach Road at breakneck speed.

When John reached his majority, his father sent him to the army, but to his great disappointment John was cashiered out for reneging on his gambling debts. When John returned to Foyle Hill, Captain Scott took the step of disinheriting him, stating that 'a son who brought the name of Scott into disgrace did not deserve to be his heir'. Captain Scott suffered his son to remain in the family home but came to regret that favour greatly because John 'Terror' Scott became wilder than ever, heading into Londonderry where the houses of ill repute were his haunts. There he could gamble and drink himself almost senseless.

Nightly he badgered his groom James McAfee to prepare the coach and horses for his foray into town. McAfee tried to warn him not to whip the horses on the steep Coach Road but John took no advice from anyone, least of all a lowly groom. McAfee told Captain Scott that his son would surely come to a sorry end but the captain only shook his head and begged McAfee to try to tame his son's wild habits. Both were dismayed that 'Terror' Scott would leave the horses untended and sweating while he caroused each night.

An opportunity came for the captain to send his son away to a tea plantation in Ceylon (Sri Lanka) where he would hold the position of manager. Despite John's reluctance the captain shipped him off in 1865 at the age of 23, and for the next three years Foyle Hill was peaceful. But John Scott did not mend his ways and he was banished from the island paradise for challenging and killing a young English officer in a duel over a woman.

Rather than being disgusted at the actions of his son, the captain boasted proudly that he had done the honourable thing as befitted the son of a military man and reinstated John as his heir. However, John's degeneracy worsened and his drinking and gambling debts increased to the despair of his father until eventually he was disinherited for good.

John met up with other young blades as wild and dissipated as himself. They called themselves 'The Hell Fire Group' and organised black ceremonies in the city. This satanic circle bought a large house on the outskirts of the city in an area known as 'Sherriff's Mountain' and held their meetings there. People of the same ilk as John 'Terror' Scott came from places as far away as Dublin and Cork.

'Walpurgis Night', 30 April, was one of the most important dates for them. On that night they held a Black Mass. In 1870, at the end of one such mass, a lightning bolt struck an old tree in the garden and it is said that Lucifer could be seen amidst the smoke. After that night they held their ceremonies around the charred tree, which they decorated with satanic symbols.

'Terror' Scott's nickname was well earned because few escaped when he lashed out in his brutish manner to his servants and indeed to anyone of an inferior status. He was particularly cruel to the groom who, when John was too drunk to come home by himself, had often retrieved him from brothels.

Rarely a day passed without John insulting him and accusing him of not doing the work that he was paid to do. The man suffered these attacks as jobs were scarce and his family depended on the cottage that came with his job.

James McAfee's young daughter Molly fell in love with John Scott's handsome looks and his devil-may-care manner, and though James tried to keep her away from the young master, John Scott somehow managed to have a 'liaison' with her unbeknownst to her father.

James heard one of the stable hands mentioning that Molly often met with John Scott when James went into Derry on errands. When her father found her crying one night he begged her to confide in him. Eventually she confessed that she was pregnant but her lover's response was to ignore her.

Her father was outraged and confronted John Scott who sneered that James's 'sweet innocent daughter' was not so innocent. James went immediately to John Scott's father to demand that his son should marry James's daughter, but the old man's aristocratic background came through. 'My son,' he said, 'cannot marry beneath him. He has a position to uphold.'

James sarcastically informed him of the terrible reputation that his son had in the city and that his name and position were already in shreds, whereupon the old man became very angry.

In the fourth month of Molly's pregnancy, old Captain Scott died. His son successfully contested the will and became master of Foyle Hill. James went once more to beg the young master to shoulder his responsibilities but he was immediately dismissed from his employ. Molly overheard their conversation and was both heartbroken and distraught with the knowledge that the man she had loved was simply a scoundrel. She wept bitter tears, lamenting that she had not listened to her father's advice. Without a word to anyone she walked to a pool beyond the house and drowned herself. One of the farmhands came upon her and ran to tell the master, who waded in and pulled her lifeless body out.

The staff almost believed that a change had come over the young master because at first he stayed at home and refused to drink, but his habits were too strongly ingrained and within a few weeks he was back to his old life.

From the moment of his daughter's death, James began to plan his revenge. He would take it in his own way and in his own time. He waited until the dark evenings came in, knowing that Scott would want to make his customary foray into town alone in preparation for Walpurgis Night.

James contrived a plan. He partially cut through the axle of the coach and when John Scott took the reins and set off, slowly at first then back to his customary breakneck speed, James followed on horseback, armed with an axe.

When 'Terror' Scott reached the steep Coach Road he tried to rein in but the sweating horses pulled against him. The coach took the curve too quickly putting such a strain on the axle that it broke, as James had known it would. The wheel fell off and the coach overturned, throwing Scott into the ditch.

Some moments later James arrived and walked over to where John 'Terror' Scott lay, dazed and injured. James waited until John Scott's eyes focused on him. As he struggled to raise himself he asked for help. James smiled grimly and said, 'I want you to know exactly why I am going to kill you. You will never, ever force yourself on another innocent girl. Now, call on your devil to save you!'

With that he took his axe and severed 'Terror' Scott's head. It is said that all of the terror that John Scott had inflicted on others throughout his life was seen on his face when the axe made its fatal blow. The head rolled for several yards down the road and thus began the haunted legend of 'The Headless Horseman'.

The beheaded ghost still haunts that road today. In the 1920s there were several sightings of John Scott's ghost by some foolhardy people who used the road by night. Several stories were related about the acrid smell that accompanied the appearance.

The Devil's chair, thought to have been carved from the tree struck by lightening during one of the Hell Fire Ceremonies.

Foyle Hill House became the Fever Hospital and visitors have reported hearing frightening voices murmuring strange incantations. After much pleading a priest finally agreed to do an exorcism. It is said that horrific screaming shook the countryside around. When the priest finished the exorcism he blessed the road with holy water and shouted, 'May you never return again!'

The ghost had been laid to rest.

Some years ago, a chair that they used in their ceremonies was found in an old barn beside the house. It is believed to be carved from the satanic tree, the centre of ceremonies on Walpurgis Night.

This chair is in the Tower Museum in the possession of the Museum and Heritage Service of Derry City Council.

The Ghost in the Bog of Lettermuck

It was a quiet night in November 1834 when the two couples left the *céilidhe* in Claudy. The men helped their wives onto the sidecar that was to take them part of the way to their homes in the townland of Lettermuck, outside Claudy. The driver urged his horse on because it was a cold night, threatening snow. There was some repartee from the back but he was in no mood to be entertained and snapped his whip, making the horse trot faster. When he came to the crossroads, Dan, one of the husbands, paid him and led the others to the shortcut through the bog. He felt no fear going across that at night for he knew it like the back of his hand. Didn't his family have a turf bank there for generations?

'Come on, this way,' he urged as the first flakes of snow fell, 'if we hurry we'll be home before it gets any worse.'

The snow eased off and they began to sing some of the Thomas Moore melodies that they'd listened to at the *céilidhe*. When Mick broke into 'Will ye come to the Bower', their pace quickened to a march and their voices rose. The women took a fit of giggles and stopped. Then their laughter turned to screams, for there, coming towards them, seeming to float on a sheet of low-lying fog, was a tall figure with an ashen face and staring eyes. The men turned at the women's screams and they too stared at the ghostly figure seeming to rise higher in the air as it approached.

'Holy Mary, what sort of a thing is it?' whispered one woman and made the sign of the cross. No one answered. The figure hovered in a ghastly halo of light and then disappeared. The darkness gathered again and they were left shocked and terrified. Without another word they rushed across the bog, heedless of the danger, and arrived at the cottage of the first couple.

'You'll stay here tonight,' Dan announced. There was no argument from the others. He poured out a drink and they downed it quickly.

'Do you think it was a ghost we saw?' asked Dan's wife. The others were silent. 'Well,' she went on, 'I think it was that man who disappeared last year. I think he was murdered and he's come back to haunt us all, for we did nothing to the three blaggards who did it.' The discussion went on far into the night as they re-lived what had happened the previous year. The *Newsletter* many years later in 1903 published the following story:

> Three brothers by the name of Matthews were the owners of a paper mill in the townland of Lettermuck outside the village of Claudy. They were known smugglers and had been fined

800/- (shillings) for a breach of the Excise Law.

An Excise Officer, Mr. James Lambkin, (locally known as Lampen) a young Scotsman, was dispatched to collect the paper excise fine but the brothers were waiting for him and a shot was heard shortly after he entered the mill.

A local woman, who said that Mr. Lambkin spoke to her as she was passing by, saw him enter the mill but he never came out. She was a key witness but she mysteriously disappeared. There was speculation at the time that she too may have been murdered. The authorities examined the possibility that the Matthews may have ground Lambkin's body to powder in the mill engine but that was never proven nor was the body recovered. All that remained was an entry in the mill book that was left unfinished.

Although they were the prime suspects of the murder of the excise man and every effort was made to recover Lambkin's body, the Grand Jury could not prosecute the Matthews brothers because of the lack of a body and they soon after shipped out to America.

Dan and Mick and their wives were not the only ones to see the ghost. More wild stories of the appearance of Lambkin's ghost circulated around and about following the murder. It was a tense time for everyone who lived in Lettermuck. In that quiet rural backwater people were genuinely afraid to go out of doors at night. After Dan and Mick's experience, few people were inclined to walk home alone over the bog at night, especially when stories of ghosts and ghouls were whispered in hushed voices at wakes and *céilidhe* nights.

The description of the ghost seldom varied. Most said that the ghost was a man, dressed in a swallowtail coat and wearing a top hat. Few saw his legs or feet because he seemed to float.

The description of the ghost was borne out when a body was uncovered in the bog of Lettermuck. The clothes, including breeches and brogues, were perfectly preserved. According to the report in *The Spectator* on 17 May 1856:

> 'Murder will out.' A skeleton has been found in a bog near Claudy near Derry. There is reason to believe that it is the skeleton of Mr Lambkin, an Excise Officer, who is believed to have been murdered twenty-four years ago. At that period two brothers named Matthews had a paper mill at Lettermuck; and they had been fined 800/. shillings for a breach of Excise-law. Mr Lambkin was seen to enter the mill; a shot was heard and Mr Lambkin was seen no more. An entry of his in the mill-book was found unfinished. The Matthews were accused of the murder of the excise man; but as every effort to recover his body had failed, the Grand Jury ignored the bill. The brothers soon afterwards emigrated to America. The bog where the skeleton was found was three-quarters of a mile from the mill. The body had been wrapped in a course woollen rug-stuff used for making common paper.

This was accepted as being James Lambkin's body. It received a Christian burial in Scotland and afterwards no further sightings of a ghost were reported, but locals are still wary about crossing the bog.

Rosemount's By-Wash

St Eugene's Girls' School on Creggan Hill in Rosemount was knocked down in 1971 but the memories linger on. It was an old grey building and by the 1950s it was much too small for the number of pupils who attended. When the new Creggan Estate came into being in 1948, the school became even more crowded with classes sometimes as large as seventy pupils.

The teachers were tremendous and pupils were given an education as wide and varied as in any private school. Nature was all around and the teachers had a fund of local folklore and very observant eyes. Sometimes the classes were actually taken on a 'nature walk' – almost unheard of in other schools in those days.

Beyond the school gate was a narrow country road, which ran alongside a rush-covered banking that led down to a hollow where a stream rushed from the Creggan reservoir to the Glen. Where the water rushed over descending steps known locally as the 'By-Wash' there was a small bridge to accommodate a road out to Hatrick's Farm.

On our walks we discovered how we received water into our houses and the teachers always made sure to point out the dangers of going near the swift runoff of water. On the farthest side of the stream, the land climbed up towards the area now known as Glenowen. This slope was densely covered with trees and even in summer it seemed dark and eerie. A large iron gate with a warning sign closed off the area from intruders, but at the side there was a hole in the hedge large enough for a child to get through.

Our teachers used the natural phenomena around to elaborate on the stories we were told in class, so any story that was set in a forest was made real, we only had to look through the classroom window to the woodland. We were always warned never to go into the forest because bad things could happen there, and never to trespass into the Garrodan, a little pathway alongside the forest, which meandered upwards toward the reservoir. (*Rodan* in Gaelic means a little road or pathway; *gar* means bent or twisted.)

All the teachers did was to create a sense of adventure in us because Mary and her friend Patsy, who lived in the 'village' of Rosemount, were hell-bent on exploring the Garrodan.

Patsy told me this story when I interviewed her about her 'ghostly' experience:

One day after school, Mary and me decided that this would be the time to go on our adventure trail. We were mad keen on playing cowboys and Indians and we thought it would be a good idea to sneak into the Garrodan to play and hunt for Indians. I told my mother that I was going to Mary's house after school and Mary told hers that she was coming to my house. We put our money together and Mary went to get a bottle of lemonade from the Baldrick's shop at the corner and I went on to the wee bridge and sat down on the wall of the bridge to wait for her.

I remember that the sun went down and a bit of a breeze began to blow and leaves were whipping up and gathering at the bridge. When the trees behind me started to sway and make a sort of moaning sound I began to lose my nerve. The forest looked too dark and scary that day to play cowboys and Indians. I decided to tell Mary that I'd changed my mind and we could just go home to my house. I was looking in the direction of Artisan Street waiting for her when I began to feel very cold so I pulled my coat around me but I was still shivering. Just then another blast of the cold air seemed to wrap itself around me and I turned to look over my shoulder, because I had this impression that the forest was coming closer. I told myself that I was being stupid, but when I looked, I got the shock of my life. There were two children, a wee boy and a girl, sort of floating up the steps and I couldn't see their feet. I thought that they were paddling in the water and called out to warn them but they weren't in the water, they just didn't seem to have any feet!

I nearly fell off the wee bridge and into the stream I was that surprised, because I hadn't seen them or heard them. I shouted again and they didn't speak, but I thought that maybe they were just nervous because I was staring at them, so I said the first thing that came into my head, and it sounded silly even to my own ears,

'Are you not cold?' I said it because they were wearing some sort of summer clothes, which I thought were a bit strange. The two of them just turned away and began to fade.

I looked away to search for Mary, and when I turned back the children were gone. I peered over the bridge on both sides but they weren't there. It seemed as if they had vanished into air. I took to my heels and ran up the road to meet Mary.

'Did you see them?' I called, 'that wee boy and girl.'

'What wee boy and girl?' Mary asked when I reached her.

'The ones down there, they were on the watery steps.'

Mary looked at me as if I was crazy.

'You were seeing things,' answered Mary and grabbed my arm, 'but my mammy said we aren't allowed to go there anyway because it's haunted.'

Rosemount's By-Wash is said to be haunted by two children who drowned there.

My heart almost missed a beat. 'Haunted!'

We turned on our heels and ran home to Mary's house. When we arrived, we were breathless and terrified. Mary's mammy listened to what I had to say and I could see that she believed me. Still, she could shed little light onto what I'd told her.

Next day when I saw Mary in school she said that her mother had asked her elderly neighbour if she knew anything. She just said that everybody in her day knew that the ghosts of two wee children who had drowned haunted the By-wash and warned us never ever to go there again.

The next day I painted a picture of the bridge and the wee boy and girl and told Miss Gallagher, my teacher, about it, but she dismissed it all as nonsense and was annoyed that we tried to go into the Garrodan after she'd warned us against it.

As far as I remember she never took us out again, but she hung my picture up on the wall and it stayed there until the summer holidays.

7

PORTENTS OF DEATH

Banshees

In the eighteenth and nineteenth century people in Ireland believed in supernatural explanations for manifestations, superstitions, cures and natural disasters. Times in Ireland were tough; people were generally trying to scrape a living out of small parcels of land. They were uneducated and open to any sort of explanation for the phenomena around them. Some saw the banshee as a devil messenger. In rural areas and in some towns the belief in banshees lingers on.

The appearance of a banshee (from the Gaelic *bean sidhe* meaning 'fairy woman') as a foreteller of death was widely believed and there are many and varied descriptions of her. She was considered to be the greatest of Irish superstitions and was sometimes described as having the body of a bird and the face of a person, sometimes even the face or a hare or of the person who would die soon. Other descriptions depicted her as an old wizened hag dressed in ragged clothes with long straggly hair flowing out behind her. Her hands were often described as talons that reached towards the house of the person who was going to die. Still another

depiction is that of a beautiful young girl who seduced the living from this life.

The sound of the banshee has variously been described as that of 100 cats wailing, faint at first and growing stronger as death becomes imminent, or of the strongest keening imaginable in the Gaelic language (from the Gaelic *ag caoineadh* meaning 'crying').

Other Portents of Death

Other portents of death were the howling of dogs, the screeching of a cat, particularly a black one, outside a person's house or the appearance of crows. A black dog walking towards a person at night is said to be the devil coming for a soul. If a picture fell from the wall, this was a premonition of death. There are too many to mention here but I will include them in my next book.

Ardmore Banshee

Diana Stevenson told me the following tale of the Ardmore Banshee:

My grandparents lived in Ardmore on the outskirts of Derry. It was a big old house and Grandma was very proud of it. She kept it well and there was always a warm welcome for Granda when he came home. He worked hard as most country doctors did in those days but he was a fit man and was seldom sick.

After dinner he usually read the paper for a while before going to bed. On this particular night, Grandma went to bed before him, and when she left to go upstairs he was perfectly well.

At some stage during the night Grandma heard an unbelievably loud screeching and wailing sound that seemed to rattle the very glass in the windows. It appeared to circle the house and was unbelievably loud just outside their window. When she looked out she could see nothing that might be causing the sound but it continued during the night, rising and falling in volume until daybreak.

Now Grandma was noted for being very sensible, certainly not a fanciful person. She was very grounded and well organised in her everyday life. Indeed Granda said that she was the one who kept them all on their toes, but that night she swore that the sound she heard was definitely the keening of the banshee. There could be no other explanation of that dreadful keening that lasted throughout the night.

Well, although Granda had been perfectly well the previous evening, he died very suddenly the following morning. Grandma maintained until the day she died that it only a banshee could create such an unearthly sound.

The Beechwood Banshee

A well-known personality in Derry worked during the day in the office of the City Cemetery, but at nights and weekends he was employed in the entertainment business.

He enjoyed meeting people and was a great listener. In Derry parlance he was 'a man of the people' who seldom forgot a name and could repeat all the stories he heard. If someone he'd ever met died, then he would visit the Wake House and go to the Requiem Mass or Service. He could also spin a good yarn.

I knew him quite well and around the time when I was gathering stories for the website www.derryghosts.com I arranged to meet him. Over a cup of tea he admitted that he had an experience that could only have been a banshee warning.

'Some people would think you strange if you confessed to anything like that but I can tell you one or two things that happened to me, as sure as I'm sitting here.'

The Beechwood Banshee is known to appear to late-night walkers on the steps at Beechwood. She is said to warn of the imminent death of a loved one.

He told me that he often walked home from work and one Sunday night, around the time when the clocks changed for winter, he was taking a shortcut up the Banking from Eastway Road to Beechwood Avenue when something very strange happened. A huge gust of wind almost blew him off his feet and he grabbed the fence at the side to steady himself. The wind seemed to gust around him and the sound was 'like a thousand cats crying'.

'I can tell you now that it was like no sound that I ever heard before. It eased off and I made it up to Beechwood when it started again like a sigh and then it rose until it nearly burst my eardrums. I can only describe that second sound like a whole orchestra playing out of tune it was so discordant. When I looked back down the Banking I saw what seemed like a figure with a dark terrible face just swirling in the mist before it disappeared. It was as quiet as a graveyard after that and the strange thing is, it was a bright moonlit night with no mist at all.'

He said, 'I know I can tell a yarn but this isn't one of them. It scared the life outta me.'

The Brandywell Banshee

Now it is believed that the banshee follows those families whose names are prefixed by Mac, Mc or O. One such elderly couple by the name of McD— lived in the Brandywell area of Derry before it was demolished in 1986. The old man took ill and his wife was very concerned that something would happen to him while she was on her own, so she asked her son Jim, who lived near Southway Road, to help. On the nights when he was at work he sent his own son, John, to stay with his grandparents, asking him to come and fetch him if his father should take a turn for the worse.

For a few weeks the boy's grandfather was stable and his grandmother, knowing that the boy missed his friends, allowed him to invite them to the house for company. She asked that they would be reasonably quiet so as not to disturb the old man. John respected his grandmother's wishes.

That night there was a terrible commotion in the back yard which John later described as 'like the sound of a thousand cats and dogs wailing and fighting outside the back door'. The boys stared at each other, clearly terrified but buoyed up by the thought that there was safety in numbers, and with a certain amount of bravado they armed themselves with pokers, tongs and coal shovels and slowly opened the back door.

The noise intensified until it became so unbearable that they dropped the weapons, covered their ears, rushed inside again and slammed the back door behind them. There was instantaneous silence. They waited for several minutes then grabbed a flashlight and after cautiously opening the door again they crept into the yard. There was nothing to be seen.

Abruptly the same screeching and discordant noises started again and seemed to come from the front of the house. When they ran to the back door it banged shut in their faces. The only way to the front was through the back gate along the dark entry lane running behind the row of houses to the end of the street.

As soon as they reached the end of the entry the rest of the boys scattered and John heard the noise at the front reach a crescendo. Conscious of his father's wish that his grandmother should not be left alone with her husband, John walked slowly to the front door, looking around him every moment, and still the noise did not abate. He spied his father hurrying towards him from the direction of his own home and ran quickly to him.

He went with his father to his grandfather's bedside where his grandmother was kneeling. The old man died a few moments later with all three at his bedside.

'Well,' his grandmother said, putting her arms around her grandson, 'he had a happy and a holy death, surrounded by those he loved. Thank you.' John started to cry and went to his father apologising for not going to fetch him. His father looked over John's head to his mother and she nodded.

'Son, something else warned me and I know you heard it too. It was a banshee and I'll be forever grateful that she allowed me to be here on time.'

True to the superstition, the banshee had warned the family whose name began with Mc.

Fulton Place Banshee

Fulton Place was a small street of twenty-three houses, built in 1895 and named after its builder, James A. Fulton. The terraced houses ran from the steep Howard Street to the perimeter wall of the St Columba's Long Tower church. The wall was high because the ancient graveyard was on the other side, on a level with the rooftops. This did not seem to bother the residents but something else most certainly did.

There are several stories about the appearance of a banshee above the roofs of the houses on the left side of the street. One of them told of a strange spectre with trailing white hair and a skull-like face who moved in ever-diminishing circles above the houses, all the while wailing like a thousand cats caterwauling.

An old man who lived in the street had been unwell for some time but wasn't known to be on the point of death. However, when several people saw her that night they knew that her appearance was a portent of death for one of the street's residents. When the screeching

Residents in Fulton Place lived in fear of the appearance of the banshee who swooped over the wall of the Long Tower church graveyard to warn of the death of one of the residents.

figure settled above the old man's house and began to wring her claw-like hands and wail even louder, they knew that someone within was going to die. Sure enough, the old man passed away but just before he did the sound of three loud knocks echoed in the street. No one had any doubt that they had seen a banshee.

The appearance of the banshee left a sense of fear in the younger people who lived in Fulton Place, especially in those families whose names began with Mac or O'. One of the families had several girls and they confessed that they were really frightened one night when they were coming home from a dance. As they turned the corner of the street, the howling and wailing began, and it was so loud that they had to cover their ears and run to their house. The banshee seemed to hover over one house in particular and the following day there was a death in that house. This may have been the same night that the old man's death was foretold.

Recently I spoke to the nephew of one of the girls, and he assured me that he had heard the story from his own father who always had to accompany his sisters home from a night out from then onwards. As soon as they reached the turn-in to Fulton Place they would hold up their hands to cover their eyes and look only at the footpath beneath their feet, such was their terror of seeing the banshee again in Fulton Place.

The street was demolished in 1977 and there have been no sightings there since.

The Banshee of Warbleshinny

Don O'Doherty was a well-known person in Derry and owned The Irish Shop in the Craft Village. He was also a very popular presenter on Radio Foyle for several years, but was best known for his role as Master of Ceremonies in St Columb's Hall.

He told me this story:

One night, when I was a lot younger, I had a strange feeling about an acquaintance of mine. I hadn't been in touch with him for a while and I decided I'd go to see him. He lived outside of Newbuildings in a townland known as Warbleshinny (from Irish, meaning 'tail of the fox').

So the following evening I got the bus to Newbuildings (I didn't have a car at the time) and then began to walk, hoping someone else would pick me up along the road. It was beginning to get dusky and, to tell you the truth, it was a bit lonely walking along there. I came to the wee narrow road that led to his place, and when I turned in I was beginning to think that I shouldn't have acted on impulse because I hadn't told him I was coming and he might not even be in.

As I was thinking these thoughts I heard a sound like muffled hooves behind me and I looked back but saw nothing on the road, only a movement of something out of the corner of my eye, near the hedge. I put it down to it being some animal. I quickened my pace but, although the trotting sounds continued, whatever it was came no closer. I was really frightened at this stage so I hurried on at a half-run. But then the sound seemed to be in front of me. I thought it was just a trick of nature because I'm a townie and I don't really know the sounds of the country.

At that moment I got the shock of my life because I saw this strange dark shadow appear on the road in front of me. It went from side to side as if it was lurching but there was enough evening light to see that there was no animal making the shadow. It looked a bit like a headless dog or a small donkey. I didn't really know what it was. It stayed in front of me all the time until I came to the gate of my friend's house. Then it disappeared.

I was never as glad in my life when I reached the house. All the lights were on and there were several people, men mostly, standing outside smoking. I just knew that something was wrong and I felt sick when I saw the black bow on the door. The men moved aside and I went in and sure enough there was a coffin along the far wall. I just stood there, quite shocked, and his wife came over to me.

'How did you hear?' she asked. 'We were just talking about you yesterday before he died and he asked me to let you know.'

'I didn't know,' I answered, 'but he was on my mind too and here I am.'

She brought me over to see his remains and when I said a prayer and

The strange shadowy creature that warned of a death.

looked at him I knew that someway, somehow, he had been in touch with me. I said nothing about my experience on the road then but several months later when I visited I told her.

She did not seem surprised.

The Graveyard Premonition

For the people who went to Mass in St Columba's church, affectionately known as the Long Tower, 8 January 1934 started off as a normal day. Children ate their breakfasts and prepared to go to the schools nearby.

Mr Quigley, a local mechanic who worked for a garage, gathered his tools and prepared to leave home. He had parked a car outside his door the previous evening. It belonged to a doctor and the mechanic needed to take it on a test drive before returning to the garage. A car was an unusual sight on the streets in the 1930s, as only doctors and the like had them, and it was essential that it be in perfect mechanical order before it was returned.

As Mr Quigley left his home off Bishop Street, his pregnant young wife called him back and with some hesitation she voiced her anxiety that something was going to happen to him. He laughed and dismissed her fears saying that he had to get back to work, but she persuaded him to stay for a few more minutes, telling him to be very careful because she had a strange uneasy feeling. He stayed and had another cup of tea, thinking that it was the latter stages of pregnancy that made her uneasy, but this meant that he returned the car a little late.

When he finally left her he drove up Bishop Street and turned left into Longtower Street. Instead of continuing that way he decided to take a shorter route and turned right onto the steeper Howard Street towards St Columb's Wells. That way he would be able to test the brakes as well.

He had driven more than halfway down the hill when he heard a tremendous crash like thunder and the car trembled and shuddered to a stop. He pulled on the handbrake and sat for a moment trying to understand what might have gone wrong with the engine. He felt the car shake again and heard a strange sound that he didn't recognise. Still puzzled, he got out and raised the car bonnet.

Unaware of the catastrophic collapse of the Longtower Graveyard wall that had happened a few hundred yards away, he tinkered with the engine, checking this and that, but he couldn't see anything amiss. He stood scratching his head and at that moment he heard a woman screaming loudly. The sound seemed to be coming from the direction of the boundary wall of the church at the far end of Fulton Place.

Neighbours came out to see what the commotion was but no one seemed to know precisely what had happened. The mechanic, satisfied that the car was fine, got in and started the engine. He was late for work and thought no more about it. Although when he reached St Columb's Wells he noticed that there was 'a bit of a fuss', he was under pressure of time and drove on.

An hour or so later the boss called him and said that his wife was on the phone. She had never done that before except when she was near her time to give birth. He had no idea what had happened and

Bystanders were appalled at the remains of the dead when the wall of the Long Tower church graveyard collapsed. (Bigger/MacDonald Collection, courtesy of NI Libraries)

Children on their way to school barely missed the collapse of the graveyard wall. Bones and coffins were evident in the landslide. (Photo Bigger/MacDonald Collection, courtesy of NI Libraries)

the first thing she said was, 'Thank God you're all right.'

'Why wouldn't I be?' he asked.

He heard her voice tremble. 'Did you not hear about the wall of the Longtower Graveyard collapsing? I thought you were dead. That's the way you always go to work.'

He assured her that he was all right. Later on, in the garage, there were bits and pieces of information coming in about the collapse and the gruesome stories of skeletons, coffins and headstones strewn about the steep brae from the Lecky Road to Holywell Street. The more he heard the more he realised that he could have been buried under the landslide if he had left home instead of staying for the cup of tea his wife had insisted upon.

On the way home he walked along the Lecky Road and when he saw the full extent of the catastrophe he was shocked. The stories that had filtered into the garage hadn't been graphic enough. The collapsed wall which he passed each day had towered about 20 feet high and ran in a semicircle shape for at least 40 yards on an incline leading to Lecky Road.

The *Derry Journal* reported that:

Graves that had lain undisturbed for perhaps two generations, were sundered, and the contents strewn on the street amid the debris of bricks and stones … Tombstones bearing the dates of the last century lay in the street beside heaps of earth and bones, while above in the cemetery could be seen portions of coffins projecting, and rails hanging over half broken graves.

In nearby Foster's Terrace, Maggie McNelis was nursing her baby when the terrifying collapse happened and she rushed out of her house with her baby in her arms and witnessed the catastrophe.

A young man called James McCloskey was standing at the corner about 10 yards away and a piece of masonry struck him.

Rose Kayne, a child who lived in the Christian Brothers' Gatehouse, described the frightful experience that she had when she saw the collapsed wall. She was on her way to school and saw a huge bank of clay with bones, skeletons and coffins sticking out of it. She ran, terrified, to the safety of the school, and when she rushed through the door a teacher took her by the hand to the biggest classroom where the head teacher was calling the attendance roll. It was only later that she heard her mother say that the teachers were checking for any missing children who may have been buried under the debris. Luckily none were and those who were absent were accounted for. All during the day as parents heard of the gruesome event they came to check that their children were all right.

When Mr Quigley reached home, his wife met him crying with relief. Later she confessed that she'd had what she thought was a bad dream the night before when she saw a huge crack opening in a wall and clay and corpses beginning to pour out of it. He was in her nightmare and she couldn't get it out of her mind, which was why she had persuaded him to delay a little longer.

He knew that his wife's strange premonition had probably saved his life. From that time on he always called into the church, knelt and said a prayer for the holy souls whose resting place had been disturbed, and he added a prayer of thanksgiving for his wife's premonition.

For years afterwards people speculated on the cause of the collapse and subsequent landslide. It was put down to the fact that the wall had been there for at least 100 years and was probably made of stone and clay, which was why it couldn't withstand the heavy rain.

Others spoke of unquiet spirits trying to escape from their 'bondage in Purgatory'. Still others spoke of hearing the banshee's wail in the area. Most thanked God saying that it was a miracle that no one had been killed.

The old streets are gone now and a new flyover passes by the wall, but even in its modernity it is still considered a 'haunted' place, especially in the dark stretches of road underneath the flyover.

8

DEATH KNOCKS

IN many parts of the world including this country, stories of death knocks abound. They are supposed to announce the imminent death of someone connected to the one who hears them. In my travels to Europe and America gathering stories I have heard many different situations when death knocks occurred, but all announced the same thing: death.

Coleraine Death Knocks

Imagine hearing three loud knocks on your door and wondering whom it could be. You aren't expecting anyone to call so early on a winter's morning, but you decide to open the door although you feel a little afraid. When you pluck up the courage, you very carefully open it, an inch at a time, expecting God knows who or what.

But there's no one there!

This was the experience of a woman in Coleraine who contacted me to tell me her story. She said that her father, who was very ill, was allowed home for Christmas from the hospital. He was pleased to be home, as were they all.

The Three Knocks are often an omen of the death of a loved one in Celtic superstition.

She rose early to get the breakfast ready for the rest of the family. She went into the kitchen and turned on the light, but as she was filling the kettle she heard three loud knocks on the back door of her house. Nervously she opened the door but no one was there.

The knocks were so loud that they woke up her two brothers, sister and mother, but her father didn't hear a thing. When the three knocks came again they thought the roof was going to cave in.

Her brothers put on their coats to go outside to investigate, but her mother, whom she later suspected knew that it was an omen, tried to stifle her fear and begged her sons not to leave the house. However, they insisted on going and walked around the house. Still they found nothing untoward.

One of them was so sure that someone was playing a trick that he got onto his bicycle and searched the streets around. While he was gone three more knocks came, this time unbelievably louder than the last times. They could make no sense of it.

Later the next day, the father was admitted into hospital urgently, and as darkness fell, he died. The woman asked herself if this could have been the grim reaper knocking on the door to come and take away her father's soul.

I told this story once in America, and two people came to me afterwards to tell the same tale of the three knocks, precisely at the time when their father, a US Marine, was killed in a shipboard accident while on manoeuvres in the Pacific.

It would seem that this is a phenomenon that happens worldwide.

The death of a parent was once heralded by three death knocks on the door of a house in Ferguson Street. The house has since been demolished.

Ferguson Street Knocks

Some years ago, a mother was in hospital quite ill. The hospital advised that the family, who were away, should come home. When they did, their mother seemed to recover a little and the family had hopes that she would be out of hospital soon. They were very attentive, visiting the hospital and being supportive to each other. One night when the mother was sleeping peacefully, the nurse said that they should go home and rest and that she would phone if there was a change, although she did not expect that there would be.

They were glad to hear some good news and when they arrived home they gathered in the living room. Just as they were about to go to bed, three loud knocks came to the window. The daughter nearest looked out but saw no one. Another three knocks sounded on the door and one of the sons went out to answer it. When he opened it there was no one there either. He went outside but the street was empty. Shortly afterwards a policeman came to tell the family that their mother had passed away. The family were aware that the knocks came at the precise time of their mother's death.

The Goodbye Knocks

In 1968 a young couple were planning to marry in Derry. They were anxiously searching for a home but the perfect one did not seem to be around.

Then they saw it.

It was a few miles outside of the city, in a secluded spot, surrounded on three sides by trees but with a beautiful view of the river to the front. To their dismay it was not for sale. Still they dreamed and kept looking for a similar place, but that one was the house that they longed to own.

They mentioned it to a friend and he happened to know the owner, so at their behest he asked him if he would sell it. The owner, an older man, wasn't keen. He explained that the house held lovely memories for him and although he couldn't manage to live there he really did not wish to sell it. He must have rethought his decision when he heard that the young couple wished to make it their first and, hopefully, only home.

They were overjoyed to buy it and after their marriage they moved in. It was a happy home and when children came along their happiness was complete. A few years after their marriage something very strange occurred.

The husband was upstairs in the front room completing some work and his wife was downstairs with the children when a loud knocking came to the front door. This was strange in itself since they had a bell and few people used the knocker. The man heard his wife go to the door but did not hear any voices. He called down to find out who had knocked.

'There was no one there,' his wife replied. Then a few moments later the same peremptory knock came. This time the man waited, knowing that his wife would speak to whoever it was, but again there were no sounds of voices. His wife called up that some children must be playing tricks and asked him to look out of the top window, which overlooked the front door, to catch sight of the pranksters.

He stood waiting to see who would come, but no one did. Yet very distinctly he heard the knocks, louder this time than before, and saw the knocker move as if being raised by an invisible hand. He was adamant that no one had approached the door. He went downstairs to his wife but they were puzzled and a little frightened by what had happened.

Just then the phone rang and when the husband answered it, it was his friend who had been instrumental in persuading the owner of the house to sell it. The phone call was to tell them that the old man had died, precisely at the time they had heard the knocks.

Rather than being frightened, they see the happening as a sign that the memories must have brought the spirit of the old man back to say goodbye to his home. Forty-five years later they are still creating their own memories in their lovely home.

9

POLTERGEISTS

A poltergeist is a presence that makes itself felt by throwing objects around, moving furniture, breaking mirrors and even touching people. A favourite but frightening activity is pulling hair or clothes when the victim least expects it. On the part of the poltergeist it may be playful, but it terrorises those who suffer from its presence.

The Collon Poltergeist

The Collon, in the Pennyburn area of the city, was considered to be almost 'out in the country' when Billy Morrison's father was young. The children had the run of the countryside around and they knew every nook and cranny.

'It was a great place to be reared,' said Mr Morrison.

The family lived in a yellow stone house in the Collon Lane for a while. A man called Gallagher owned it and the Morrisons were delighted to have a house for themselves rather than having to share a place with another family.

It soon became apparent why few families stayed long in that house when strange things began to happen at all hours of the day and night. Crockery, chairs and many other things were thrown about and Mrs Morrison was terrified that one of the children would be hurt.

There seemed to be no pattern in these explosions of activity but it was a petrifying experience for those who lived there. At first, neighbours were reluctant to speak about it, but eventually they told the Morrisons that there was a poltergeist in residence in the form of a big red-headed, bearded man.

The Morrison family tried to find another place to live, and in the meantime they blessed the house and burned holy candles, but the poltergeist was not to be moved. It finally drove them out as soon as they found another house.

Cottage Row Poltergeist

Before the redevelopment took place in Rosemount in 1976 there was a street that ran from Creggan Road to Park Avenue. Forty-two houses were built there between 1873 and 1896. It was strange in that each side had a different name. One side was North Street and the other side of twenty houses was named Cottage Row. It was one of the older streets in 'The Village', as Rosemount was known, and the area still had a rural ambience. As in most rural areas, ghost stories, tales of fairies and superstitions were handed down. One of the strangest stories was that of a poltergeist in a house in Cottage Row.

In the 1920s John, his wife and three children were preparing to move into a house there. They were delighted when they received the keys because there were few houses available for renting. They moved in their meagre furniture and the husband set about painting it. He wanted the children's bedroom to look nice for Christmas so he decided to begin decorating that room first.

It had a sloped ceiling and a skylight, and while he painted the ceiling the children jumped on the bed and played around. When he stooped to dip the paintbrush in the tin of paint, a hairbrush just missed his head, bounced off the ceiling and fell into the paint tin, splashing the paint all around. He turned angrily and demanded to know which one of the children had thrown the brush. They stood wide-eyed, staring at him and pointing behind him, 'She did,' they chorused. The father turned but saw nothing. He asked them once more which one of them had thrown the brush. Again they denied doing it and he ordered them out of the room. He called to his wife to see to them until he cleaned up the mess.

When he went back into the room he began to wipe up the paint from the floor with an oilcloth but each time he wiped the paint up it reappeared again in a different place. He began to feel afraid, and was searching his mind for a logical explanation when the tin of paint raised itself in the air and was flung against the wall with such force that it made a deep gouge. As the paint slowly slid down the wall it spelt out the word 'GO'.

Quietly he closed the bedroom door and went downstairs. The children were sitting quite subdued at the table and his wife was asking what they had done to annoy their father. When he entered he motioned her to follow him out of the kitchen.

'There's something strange going on in this house, take the children and go to your mother's.' When she demurred he said, 'I'll explain it all later but leave now.'

After she left, he walked down to the cathedral and asked to see one of the priests. He explained what had happened and the priest, who was well into his later years, was slightly sceptical. However, when he saw how upset John was he accompanied him to the house where he was confronted with further damage in the living room and kitchen. Wallpaper was torn off the wall, pictures were emptied out of boxes and the glass smashed, all except one – a Sacred Heart picture with the family's names inscribed.

The priest said nothing but put on his stole and walked to the bedroom with John following. When they entered the room an almighty racket began and the bed was flung from one side of the room to the other. The priest prayed a blessing loudly and asked John to hold the crucifix in front of him. As he prayed he descended the stairs slowly and sprinkled holy water. He walked around the house, blessing each room and praying. When he reached the back door he asked John to open it, but it refused to budge, and on the priest's instructions John touched it with the crucifix. It crashed open. The priest walked to the end of the yard and again John opened the back gate. The priest continued praying for several minutes and then asked John to close the gate.

When they re-entered the house he said, 'You will not be troubled again but be aware that someone needs your prayers.'

John could see that the old priest was drained and he accompanied him back to the parochial house.

The family moved in, and true to the words of the priest, they were not troubled again.

BBC Radio Foyle – Ghost or Poltergeist?

Eamon Friel recalled the following tale:

I've never been convinced about ghosts and I've never had any reason to be until quite recently. I only remember ghosts being an issue in my family once. I spent my school summer holidays each year in County Mayo. My mother was from rural Mayo and some cousins of ours, who lived across the river, had trouble of some sort in their house. They built a new house but the issue seemed to have followed them there. Eventually they moved to a farm far away in Wicklow. They didn't speak much about their bother, reticent as country people often are, but it was obvious to my mother that they were seriously disturbed by something. I thought myself at the time that perhaps they were letting their imagination run away with them. I'm not so sure about that now.

I started working for the BBC in the mid-1980s, first as a topical songwriter and then as a presenter of mainly music shows, based at Radio Foyle. It would have been in the later 1990s that I first heard word of a Radio Foyle ghost. I regret to say that I didn't pay that much attention. Apparently a couple of people in the newsroom had had peculiar experiences in the studios. I didn't think much of it. Radio Foyle to my mind at the time was an unlikely haunt for a ghost. It was a new building opened in the 1980s, a most unlikely setting for a Hammer horror picture. One of the security men did say to me that he had seen a figure in Studio 1B in the early hours of the morning. He went to investigate but there was nobody there. He didn't seem too worried. He said he must have been mistaken. The ghost thing faded after a while in the station.

One night I was presenting the *Thursday Late Show* on Radio Ulster. This would have been in the early 2000s. I was in the other studio at Foyle called 1A. I still play quite a bit of vinyl because it contains great music that will never make its way on to CD. It was about 11 o'clock at night. The show was about halfway through. The next record was a vinyl album track and I set it up for broadcast in the usual way. I put the record on the turntable and checked that the speed was set correctly. I placed the needle just before the track I wanted and listened on pre-fade till I found exactly where it began. I switched off the pre-fade button on the desk and moved the record back a little manually so that it didn't start with a whirr. It was set up, ready to go. I introduced the song and then opened the fader. Nothing happened. I looked round at the record player and it had been switched off!

There I was live on air and quite startled! I'd no choice but to continue, so I apologised and went to a CD I had already set up. Then I checked the record player by switching it on again.

It was working perfectly. There is no way I could have switched it off. The circular off switch was at the top of the machine, quite a distance away from where I had been working. I mentioned what had happened to a few people but the general reaction was that I must have inadvertently switched the machine off, and that's more or less how I came to view the incident, even though I didn't really believe it.

In January 2015 Madeline McCully emailed me to tell me she was compiling a book about Derry hauntings. She was contacting me because I'd told her some time before about my peculiar experience in Studio 1A. Madeline's email arrived on a Wednesday. The following Saturday I went into Radio Foyle early, about 8 a.m., to prepare my Radio Ulster show that evening. At around 10.30 p.m. I took a break. There's a

piano in what's known as the middle cubicle. I went in. There was no one in the room. It's the room between 1A and 1B. Although it is called the cubicle it is bigger than either of the two studios. It's used by bands for live performance or for round-table discussions involving numbers that neither of the two studios can cope with. The piano was closed and there was a black plastic clip sitting on it, so I removed it and placed it on the big round table behind me because it might have rattled when I was playing. The clip is used to pin a microphone lead to the microphone stand. It's made of hard plastic and it's a couple of inches long. I opened the piano, sat down and played for about ten minutes.

Suddenly something flew past my head on my left and hit the piano with a loud sound, then dropped to the ground by my left foot. I looked round. There was nobody there. I bent down and picked up the object. It was a plastic clip. I turned round again. The clip I had left on the table was gone. It is important to stress that I did not feel afraid. Why, I don't know. I was very surprised though because there is simply no explanation for what happened. All I can say is that Madeline's email and the incident three days later have to be connected in some way. Something or somebody was telling me, 'I'm still here'.

Eamon Friel at the piano where he experienced poltergeist activity.

BIBLIOGRAPHY AND FURTHER READING

Boyle, D., *Half-hanged McNaghten* (Guildhall Press, 1993)

Bonner, B., *Derry: An Outline History of the Diocese* (Foilseachain Naisiunta Teoranta, 1982)

DCC, Heritage & Museum Services, *Atlantic Memorial 1939–1945* (Derry City Council)

Bryson, J.G., *The Streets of Derry* (Guildhall Press, 2001)

Byrne, P.F., *Tales of the Banshee* (Cork: Mercier Press, 1987)

Byrne, P.F., *Irish Ghost Stories* (Cork: Mercier Press, 1965)

Burrow, J., *Map of Londonderry* (London: J. Burrow & Co., 1970)

Carson, W., *Vanishing Derry* (Donegal: Donegal Democrat Ltd, 1978)

Carson, W., *Yesterday* (Donegal: Donegal Democrat Ltd, 1982)

Colby, Col. R.E., *Ordnance Survey of the County of Londonderry* (Dublin: Hodges & Smith, 1837)

Cooke, S., *The Maiden City and the Western Front* (Dublin: Morris & Co., 1957)

Craig, P. (ed.), *The Oxford Book of Ireland* (Oxford University Press, 1998)

Cunningham, P., *Derry Memories* (Guildhall Press, 2007)

Curry, F., *War at Sea: A Canadian Seaman in the North Atlantic* (Lugus; Toronto, 1990)

Dunne, J.J., *Haunted Ireland, her Romantic and Mysterious Ghosts* (Belfast: Apple Tree Press, 1977)

Gallagher, C., *Acorns and Oak Leaves* (Derry: Oakleaf Press, 1981)

Hamilton, R., *100 Years of Derry* (Belfast: Blackstaff Press, 1999)

Hughes, S., *City on the Foyle* (Derry: Ogmios Press, 1984)

Lacey, B., *Discover Derry* (Dublin, The O'Brien Press Ltd, 1999)

Lysaght, P., *The Banshee: The Irish Death Messenger* (Dublin: O'Brien Press, 1986)

Hurrell, K. & Lewis, B.K., *The Unexplained – A Source Book* (Flame Tree Publishing, 2003)

McCormack, K., *Ken McCormack's Derry* (Dublin: Londubh Books, 2010)

McFadden, V., *Island City* (Leberg Press: 2012)

McGuinness, M. & Downey, G., *Creggan: More than a History* (Guildhall Press, 2000)

McMahon, S. (ed.), *A History of County Derry* (Dublin: Gill & McMillan, 2004)

McMahon, S., *A Derry Anthology*
(Belfast: Blackstaff Press, 2002)

Mitchell, B., *A City Invincible*
(Grocers' Hall Press, 1990)

Mitchell, B., *On the Banks of the Foyle*
(Belfast: Friar's Bush Press,1999)

O'Farrell, P., *Irish Ghost Stories*
(Dublin: Gill & McMillan, 2004)

Rowan, A., *North-West Ulster: The Buildings
of Ireland* (Penguin Books, 1979)

Seymour & Neligan, *True Irish Ghost
Stories* (Dublin, Allen Figgis Ltd, 1969)

Ulster Architectural Heritage Society, *In and
Near the City of Derry* (UAHS, 1970)

WELB & LS & NW Archaeological &
Historical Society *Derry – Around the
Maiden City* (2003)

Woods, F., *Memories of Derry Quay*
(Derry: Yes Publications, 2007)

Newspapers

Derry Journal
Londonderry Sentinel
Coleraine Chronicle,

Archived
Irish Newsletter
Spectator

Periodicals

Waterside Voices
Ireland's Own
Ireland's Eye

Websites

www.rsai@rsai.ie
www.derryghosts.com
www.nationaltrust.org.uk,
www.nooseornecklace.com
www.limavady.gov.uk

Visit our website and discover thousands of
other History Press books.

www.thehistorypress.ie